Developing Li
POETRY COMPENDIUM

PHOTOCOPIABLE TEACHING RESOURCES
FOR LITERACY

ages
7–11

Christine Moorcroft

Series consultant Ray Barker

A & C BLACK

Contents

Ages 9–10

Ages 10–11

Acknowledgements

The author and publishers are grateful for permission to reproduce the following:

'A Piper' by Seumus O'Sullivan reproduced by kind permission of Mrs Frances Sommerville from *Collected Poems* (Orwell Press, Dublin); 'Sea Timeless Song' reproduced with permission of Curtis Brown Ltd, London, on behalf of Grace Nichols; 'Cats' by Eleanor Farjeon from *Blackbird has spoken* published by Macmillan, reproduced with permission of David Higham Associates Ltd, London; 'Sing a Song of People' reproduced with permission of the Lois Lenski Covey Foundation Inc © 1965 Lois Lenski; 'Cargoes' and 'Reynard the Fox' by John Masefield reproduced with permission of the Society of Authors as the Literary Representatives of the Estate of John Masefield; 'The Writer of This Poem' reprinted by permission of PFD on behalf of Roger McGough © 1983 Roger McGough; 'Morning' by Grace Nichols reproduced with permission of Curtis Brown Ltd, London, on behalf of Grace Nichols © 1998 Grace Nichols; 'Dandelion Time' from *The Works* (Macmillan), reproduced with permission of Sue Cowling © 2000 Sue Cowling; 'The Black Pebble' and 'The Snitterjipe' © 1973, 1994 James Reeves from *Complete Poems for Children* (Heinemann), reprinted by permission of the James Reeves Estate; 'in Just' by E. E. Cummings is reprinted from *Complete Poems 1904–1962*, by E. E. Cummings, edited by George J. Firmage, by permission of W. W. Norton & Company © 1991 by the Trustees for the E. E. Cummings Trust and George James Firmage; 'The Song of Life' by Véronique Tadjo, reproduced with permission of the author; 'The Listeners' by Walter de la Mare, reproduced by permission of the Literary Trustees of Walter de la Mare and the Society of Authors as their representative; 'Write-A-Rap Rap' by Tony Mitton © Tony Mitton 2000, from *The Works*, chosen by Paul Cookson, Macmillan, 2000; 'The Visitor' by Ian Serraillier reproduced by permission of Anne Serraillier; 'Leisure' by W. H. Davies reproduced by permission of Mr K. P. Griffin on behalf of the Will trust of Mrs H. M. Davies; 'Song of the Street' Poems and melodies from Iceland, CD, published by Torfi Olafson, 1997; 'Haiku (Ice on the Front Step)' © Patricia V. Dawson, reproduced by permission of Maria Dawson and Patricia V. Dawson; 'Silver Aeroplane' © 2000 John Foster from *The Works*, chosen by Paul Cookson, Macmillan, 2000, included by permission of the author; 'Dust' © 1979 John Mole, first published in *Once there were Dragons* (Andre Deutsch); 'Eye Sore' reprinted by permission of PFD on behalf of Roger McGough © 1983 Roger McGough; 'They're Fetching in Ivy and Holly' © Charles Causley, from *Collected Poems for Children*, published by Macmillan, reproduced by permission of David Higham Associates; 'In This City' © 1961 Alan Brownjohn.

Every effort has been made to trace copyright holders and to obtain their permission for use of copyright material. The authors and publishers would be pleased to rectify in future editions any error or omission.

Published 2008 by A & C Black Publishers Limited
38 Soho Square, London W1D 3HB
www.acblack.com

ISBN: 978-1-4081-0051-6

Copyright text © Christine Moorcroft, 2001, 2008
Ages 7–8
Copyright illustrations © Michael Evans and Leon Baxter, 2001
Ages 8–9
Copyright illustrations © Susan Hutchison, 2001
Ages 9–10/Ages 10–11
Copyright illustrations © Bridget Dowty, 2001
Copyright cover illustration © Sean Longcroft, 2008

The author and publishers would like to thank Ray Barker, Madeleine Madden, Kim Pérez and Julia Tappin for their advice in producing this series of books.

A CIP catalogue record for this book is available from the British Library.

Printed in Great Britain by Caligraving Ltd, Thetford, Norfolk.

This book is produced using paper that is made from wood grown in managed, sustainable forests. It is natural, renewable and recyclable. The logging and manufacturing processes conform to the environmental regulations of the country of origin.

Introduction

'If we know what we are doing when we teach poetry then we shall be secure: the rest of our work in English will follow by implication. Poetry is language used for its deepest and most fully exact purposes.'

David Holbrook, *English For Maturity*, Cambridge University Press, 1961

Many teachers are somewhat hesitant about introducing poetry into their classroom, perhaps remembering their own experiences in secondary school, where poetry was 'something to study' and the material related to the cultural tradition of poetry. Often poetry was seen as 'difficult' and old-fashioned. In the public domain it is often seen as something 'odd' and outside the current of normal life.

This reluctance should not be a problem in primary school. Young children enjoy poems; they enjoy reading them, talking about them and writing them. They enjoy the rhythms and sounds and patterns of poetry. Contemporary, experimental poets have helped in breaking down barriers around poetry, writing directly for young children in a language and style they can enjoy directly, but children's enjoyment is not limited to comic subjects and rhyme. Children need to be challenged by a range of subjects, forms and language. Poetry can offer a useful 'door to the past'. Of all art forms, it is 'most able to adapt itself to other epochs and other readerships.' (Laurence Lerner, *Reconstructing Literature*, Blackwell, 1983) A distinctive characteristic of poetry is its accessibility to all sorts of learners. Poems offer a

range of choice, and are 'small' enough to be used in all classrooms for any amount of time.

Poems work differently from stories, creating effects and evoking responses which may overlap with the art of the story, but which are often peculiar to the nature of poetry.

- They are immediate; children will often 'get it' or not, more quickly. If some children don't 'get it', this means that poems will have to be read more than once.

- Children sense there is a 'riddling' quality to poems – in the way words are used or the way they are laid out on the page.

- Poems remind us about the creativity of language and young children are open enough to grasp that reader and poet meet on common ground – the ground of a shared language.

- Poems are 'multi-meaning' and there is not often a right answer to 'meaning'.

- Our responses to poetry are less linear than to a story. Poems are presented in a huge variety of ways and their job is not often to answer the question, 'What happens next?' Readers move around 'within' the poem for emotional impact or meaning.

- Poems provide 'experiences' and these are gained through a mixture of: the language used, the form, feelings communicated, detail used.

- Poetry was originally an oral form – stories and word-fun told and shared by others. It is not strictly a reading and writing activity. Poetry should be listened to as well – and often performed.

- Children can create poems more easily than a story and so achieve success. But poetry is not a one-off inspirational activity. It is something developmental and structured. You can create poems from ideas and then develop appropriate language and pattern around lists, from comparisons, from sounds, from stories.

Poetry activities in this series:

- are categorised to help you with planning – see the charts on pages 10, 40, 71 and 101.

- are linked to the Primary Framework for Literacy.

- cover a wide range of forms and types of poetry – from a range of cultures and eras.

Using the activity sheets

Few resources are needed besides scissors, glue, word-banks and simple dictionaries. Access to ICT resources – computers, DVD, video, digital cameras, tape-recorders – would also be useful at times.

Brief teaching notes are provided at the bottom of each page – these can be masked before photocopying. More detailed notes and suggestions can be found in the **Notes on the activities** preceding each age group's activity sheets.

Most of the activity sheets end with a challenge (**Now try this!**) which reinforces and extends the children's learning and provides the teacher with an opportunity for assessment. These more challenging activities might be appropriate for only a few children; it is not expected that the whole class should complete them although many will be able to do so as a shared guided activity. On some pages there is space for the children to complete the extension activities, but for others they will need a notebook or a separate sheet of paper.

Ten things to think about when teaching poetry

Do you:

1 have a classroom containing a range of poetry resources, including anthologies, ICT, posters?

2 provide a range of challenging approaches and frameworks to writing that extend children's appreciation of poetry?

3 encourage children to look for writing opportunities in their own lives?

4 see writing as a process: gathering ideas, drafting, sharing and presentation?

5 vary approaches to writing in your class: pairs, groups, individuals, etc.?

6 have confidence that the class can be a critical audience for the work of others?

7 encourage children to read aloud and perform poems?

8 read aloud poetry to the class yourself on a regular basis?

9 see awareness of audience as essential to a piece of writing and find audiences for the work of the class, e.g. younger children, parents?

10 offer a range of possibilities for presenting material, e.g. ICT, creating anthologies, and for publication, e.g. the Internet?

Assessment

The monitoring and assessment of poetry will depend upon the learning objectives set within any specific lesson; it is important to be clear about the nature of the aspect of poetry to be assessed. Teachers will also take into consideration some general principles, for example:

- Are you assessing the understanding of a principle, e.g. rhyme, simile – or are you assessing the quality of a written poem?

- In one sense, poetry is about the unassessable. The best poetry is unexpected, surprising and unpredictable.

- Any assessment needs to involve the reader and the audience, too.

- Is it more important that the child is developing increasing confidence in handling language or looking at the world in a more thoughtful, individual way?

Other activities in the series are ideal for the collection of evidence over the year and for the children to assess their own and each other's poetry. It is not expected that teachers will be able to assess all the class at any one time. It may be best to focus on a small group of children each week, although it may be possible to use the objectives for whole-class monitoring with certain activities. There should be opportunities for making comments and monitoring the children's ability in other subject areas over the week. However, all the information should be assimilated for an end-of-year summary which will enable easier transition and target-setting.

Notes on the activities

The notes below expand upon those provided at the bottom of the activity pages. They give ideas and suggestions for making the most of the activity sheet, including suggestions for the whole-class introduction, the plenary session or for follow-up work using an adapted version of the sheet. To help teachers to select appropriate learning experiences for their pupils, the activities are grouped into units in line with the Primary Framework for Literacy, but the pages need not be presented in the order in which they appear, unless stated otherwise.

Unit 1: Poems to perform

The poems in this section should be read aloud by the children, either taking turns during the introductory session or in groups; give them opportunities to experiment with different ways of reading the poems aloud (including different numbers of voices for different parts of the poem), and encourage them to look out for repeated parts, such as choruses, which could be read by the whole group.

Poetry in action: 1 and **2** (pages 12–13). Practise before you read the poem aloud to the children. You will probably quite naturally read it with the rhythm of the piper first standing still, tuning up and then beginning to play a tune – becoming livelier as it progresses, then with the rhythm of people coming out of their doors and dancing to the tune. Similarly, you will notice the fairly quiet beginning with the

volume increasing along with the tempo – and then becoming quiet again in the last line. After the children have listened to the poem, ask them to listen again and to get up and enact the scene, thinking about how quickly or slowly they move and what kinds of movements the poem makes them want to make. Focus on the way in which punctuation helps you to read the poem. Some lines run straight into the next one without a pause: ask the children to identify those lines as well as the pauses. Ask them also to notice the effect of the repetition of 'away' in line 3, the repetition of 'and' at the beginnings of lines 6, 7 and 8 and the way in which rhyme contributes to the rhythm. The children should notice that the poem begins with a quiet street in which a piper takes out his pipe and then plays one or two notes before launching into the tune which draws everyone outdoors until the street is full of people dancing to the rhythm of an Irish jig. At the end the piper stops playing and it is as if all the people suddenly go back to their ordinary everyday activities: the street is quiet once more. The children could refer to their descriptions of scenes when enacting the poem and even use them as the basis of stage directions for others to enact it.

Market poem (page 14). This provides the beginning of, and a framework for, writing a poem for the children to complete and then perform. Encourage them first to make notes of anything which might be sold at a market and then to look for rhyming pairs of words and to add descriptions which fit the rhythm. Other words which might help them include: good strong nails/plastic pails, garden tools/wooden stools and chocolate flakes/fairy cakes as well as half-rhymes like sweet and sour chicken/patterns for knitting.

Spooky poem (page 15). This activity concentrates on the effects of words. It could be linked with sentence structure work on adjectives and verbs. A source of spooky poems suitable for this age group is *Young Hippo Spooky Poems* compiled by Jennifer Curry (Hippo, 1998); classic poems which are also suitable include 'The Ghosts' High Noon' (W. S. Gilbert), 'The Witches' Chant' (from Shakespeare's *Macbeth*), 'The Ghoul' (Jack Prelutsky) and 'The Visitor' (Ian Seraillier).

On and on (page 16). This page provides an example of a poem in which words are repeated to create an effect (the rhythm of the sea). One group of children could repeat quietly 'sea timeless' while another group (simultaneously) reads the entire poem, with the whole class joining in the last four lines of each verse.

Day and night (page 17). Here is an example of a poem in which words are repeated to create an effect (of the day waking up). Compare its lively opening with that of 'A Piper' (page 12). It presents the day as if it is human: this lays a foundation for later work on personification. In groups, the children could discuss how they would perform the daybreak and nightfall poems and what movements they might include to point up the contrasts between them.

Travel rhymes (page 18). *Possible answers to the main activity*: swim to Lymm, ski (or flee) to Dundee, sail to Hale, speed to the Tweed, row to Stowe, ride (or slide) to Hyde, skate to Margate and crawl to Porthcawl. *Possible answers to the extension activity*: walk to York (or Cork or Dundalk), dance to France, fly to Skye (or Rye) and tear to Ware. The children could also look for places which rhyme

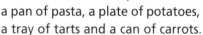

with scamper, skid, trot, roll, hop, skip, run, jig, race, skate, leap, wade, paddle, drive and so on. Once they have completed the activity, they could choose some of the travel verbs, practise miming them in their groups and then recite and perform them to the rest of the class in the plenary session.

Monday's child (page 19). This page gives the children a model on which to base a simple rhyming poem. The rhyme-finder provides pairs of rhyming words from which the children can choose; encourage them to think up others of their own. Ask volunteers to perform their new versions of the poem to the rest of the class.

Heavy or light (page 20). This activity draws attention to the effects of words and helps the children to recite poems with appropriate intonation and stress. The children could also list words which sound rough or smooth, soft or hard.

Alliterative allsorts (page 21). Here the focus is on the main consonant sounds in words. The children should notice the effect of the repetition of these sounds in poem recitals. They could look for other examples of alliteration in poems they read. *Possible answers*: a bunch of bananas, a bottle of beer, a hunk of ham, a dish of damsons, a chunk of cheese, a cup of cocoa, a lump of lard, a basket of bread, a mug of milk, a slice of sausage, a bowl of berries, a litre of liquid, a pan of pasta, a plate of potatoes, a tray of tarts and a can of carrots.

Still as a post and tall as a spire and **Comparisons** (pages 22–23). These activities could be linked with work on similes. The children could make collections of comparisons or similes they come across in their reading. They could also suggest ways of expressing comparisons in performances: using appropriate intonation, hand gestures and body movements to suggest size or height and facial expressions to show fear or joy or sorrow and so on.

The same but different: 1 and **2** (pages 24–25). These two poems are about the same subject, treated quite differently. Ask the children to read them aloud.

What do they notice? Draw out that the first poet seems to like cats and presents them as taking very little notice of people – doing just as they like, in fact ('*They* don't care!'). The second poet presents the cat as hating people and as evil (with phrases such as 'the hate of a million years', 'snaky tail' and 'demon's song'). For a class anthology the children could cut out cat shapes on which to write poems they come across about cats.

Unit 2: Shape poetry and calligrams

These pages introduce shape poems and invite the children to explore the effects of layout on a poem and the ways in which the shape can be an integral part of the poem's meaning.

Catch the hatchet! and **Onomatopoeia collections** (pages 26–27). Ask the children why they think the shapes on page 26 have sharp points. Discuss what shape would be best to write smooth-sounding words in. Useful words include batch, crotchet, crutch, ditch, each, fetch, hatch, hotch-potch, ketchup, latch, match, patch, ratchet, scratch, stitch, touch and watch. For the extension activity on page 27, ask the children to draw an appropriate shape to frame their list of onomatopoeic words.

Splash poem, **Shape sentences** and **Word shapes** (pages 28–30). These activities explore poems and poetic sentences whose shape reflects their subject and provide frameworks on which the children can write their own. Examples (from *The Works*, published by Macmillan) include 'AND IT'S A…' (Rita Ray), 'The Shape I'm In' (James Carter) and 'Rhythm Machine' (Trevor Harvey). Tony Mitton, Coral Rumble and John Foster also write shape poems.

Calligrams (page 31). Here the words themselves are formed in shapes which express something about the subject-matter. The activity provides ideas to help the children to use their imaginations to create their own calligrams.

Unit 3: Language play

In this section the children are encouraged to enjoy nonsense poems and poems which explore words and ideas, and to play tricks with tongue-twisters and riddles.

Ptarmigans and pterodactyls (page 32). This activity invites the children to explore the sounds of words with silent letters and to make up new ones. It develops their ability to recognise, and create their own, humour with word-play.

Word jokes (page 33). Examples with which to introduce the activity include words whose letters are exchanged and others whose opening sounds are exchanged but with different spellings: for example, jelly beans/belly jeans, skipping rope/ripping scope, motor bike/boater Mike, front door/grunt four, bus fare/fuss bear, note book/boat nook, phone call/cone fall. This activity could be linked with work on grapheme and phoneme correspondence. *Answers*: mad bunny, cat-flap, cold ghost, making toast.

Absurd words (page 34). Other words with more than one meaning which the children could explore include eye, foot, head. They could make up jokes about the words: for example, a needle gives sharp looks with its eye, the bed stamped its foot, the pin nodded its head. *Answers*: the bonnet of a car, a car boot, a disc jockey, a daffodil bulb, fingernails, the tongue of a shoe, the mouth of a tunnel, the wings of a building, a cricket bat and a fish finger.

Legs riddle (page 35). This is an old riddle about a man or woman who sits on a three-legged stool with a leg of lamb (or other meat) in a bag; a dog or cat runs off with the meat, the man or woman jumps up and throws the stool after the animal and makes it bring back the meat. Some children might need help: for example, 'think of things with three legs/two legs…' and so on.

Twister (page 36). This page gives extracts from two old tongue-twisters which are difficult to read slowly, let alone quickly. Discuss the phonemes which cause the difficulty (the sequence of 's' and 'th' sounds). The children might need to be reminded of the different ways of spelling the 's' phoneme: 's', 'ss', 'ce'.

Learning objectives

The following chart shows how the Ages 7–8 activity sheets (pages 12–36) match the learning objectives addressed by the Year 3 units in the Poetry block of the Primary Framework for Literacy. (Where a page number is shown in bold type, this indicates the learning objective is the main focus of the activity.)

Objectives	Unit 1: Poems to perform	Unit 2: Shape poetry and calligrams	Unit 3: Language play
Speaking			
Choose and prepare poems or stories for performance, identifying appropriate expression, tone, volume and use of voices and other sounds	12–14, **24**		32, 36
Sustain conversation, explain or give reasons for their views or choices		26, 29	34
Group discussion and interaction			
Actively include, and respond to, all members of the group	24		
Drama			
Identify and discuss qualities of others' performances, including gesture, action, costume	12, 13, 24		
Word structure and spelling			
Spell high- and medium-frequency words	14, 18, 19, 21, 23	26–29	35, 36
Recognise a range of prefixes and suffixes, understanding how they modify meaning and spelling, and how they assist in decoding long, complex words	15		33
Spell unfamiliar words using known conventions including phoneme/grapheme correspondences and morphological rules	15, 18, 21–23	28, 31	32–34, 36
Understanding and interpreting texts			
Explore how different texts appeal to readers using varied sentence structures and descriptive language	12–14, **16**, **17**, **20**, 21, 23, 24, **25**	26, 29–31	32, 35, 36

Objectives	Unit 1: Poems to perform	Unit 2: Shape poetry and calligrams	Unit 3: Language play
Engaging with and responding to texts			
Identify features that writers use to provoke readers' reactions	**12**, **13**, **14**, 16, 17, 20, 22–25	30, 31	**32, 33, 34, 35, 36**
Creating and shaping texts			
Make decisions about form and purpose, and identify success criteria for their writing		28, 29, **30**, 31	36
Select and use a range of technical and descriptive vocabulary	**15**, 16, 17, **18**, **19**, 20, **21**, **22**, **23**	26–31	32, 35, 36
Use layout, format, graphics, illustrations for different purposes		**26, 27, 28, 29, 31**	33
Text structure and organisation			
Signal sequence, place and time to give coherence	12, 13, 17, 19		
Sentence structure and punctuation			
Show relationships of time, reason and cause, through subordination and connectives	12, 13, 16		
Compose sentences using adjectives, verbs and nouns for precision, clarity and impact		26, 29	33
Presentation			
Write with consistency in size and proportion of letters and spacing within and between words, using the correct formation of handwriting joins	12–23, 25	26–31	32–36
Develop accuracy and speed when using keyboard skills to type, edit and redraft	14, 15, 19		36

A Piper

A piper in the streets today

Set up, and tuned, and started to play,

And away, away, away on the tide

Of his music we started; on every side

Doors and windows were opened wide,

And men left down their work and came,

And women with petticoats coloured like flame.

And little bare feet that were blue with cold,

Went dancing back to the age of gold,

And all the world went gay, went gay,

For half an hour in the street today.

Seumus O'Sullivan

- **Number the lines in the poem 1 to 11.**
- **Imagine the street. In the boxes, write what you can see and hear.**

Just before the poem begins
What do you think the street looks like? Is anyone there?

In lines 1 and 2
Who is there? Doing what? What can you hear?

Teachers' note Read the poem aloud. It begins hesitantly, with a few notes of the pipe (note the commas); the rhythm of a jig develops in the third line and ends on the last line (when the people stop dancing and return to their work). Ask the children to imagine the poem as a series of scenes in a play or film. What would they see and hear? Continued on page 13.

Developing Literacy Poetry Compendium: Ages 7–11 © A & C BLACK

Poetry in action: 2

In lines 3 to 5

What do you see happening?
What do you hear?

In line 6

Who comes out into the street?
What do you hear?

In line 7

Who comes out into the street now?
Wearing what? Who is in the street now?

In line 8

Who comes out?
Who is in the street now?

In lines 9 to 11

What can you see and hear in the street?

After the end of the poem

How does the scene change? What do all the people do?

Teachers' note The children should begin this activity on page 12. As an extension activity, some children might be able to write stage directions for enacting the poem while it is read aloud.

Developing Literacy
Poetry Compendium:
Ages 7–11
© A & C BLACK

Market poem

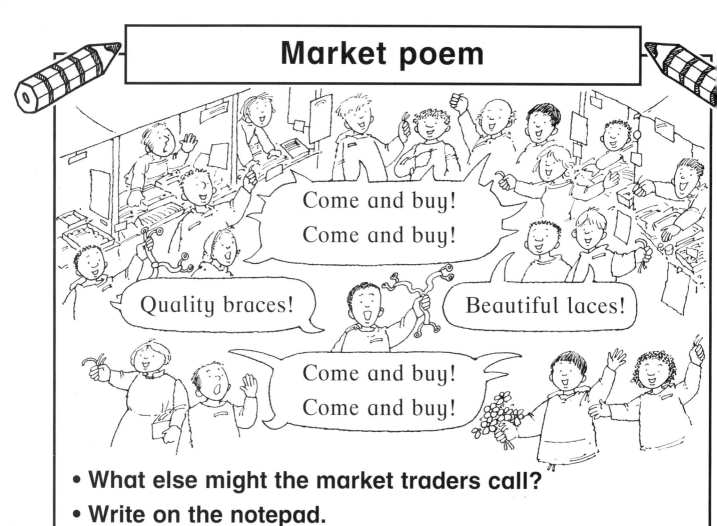

- **What else might the market traders call?**
- **Write on the notepad.**

knives and forks
bottles and corks

freshly-baked ham
strawberry jam

- **Write three verses for the market poem.**

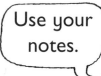

Use your notes.

- **Perform the poem with your group.**

Now try this!

Teachers' note Read the verse to the children and ask them for suggestions on how it could be performed by a group: how many people should read each line (the same person or different ones?) and how many should read the chorus? Invite a group to demonstrate their ideas. The children should use a computer to type, edit and redraft their new verses.

**Developing Literacy
Poetry Compendium:
Ages 7–11
© A & C BLACK**

Spooky poem

- **Write adjectives and verbs which make the old house seem spooky.**

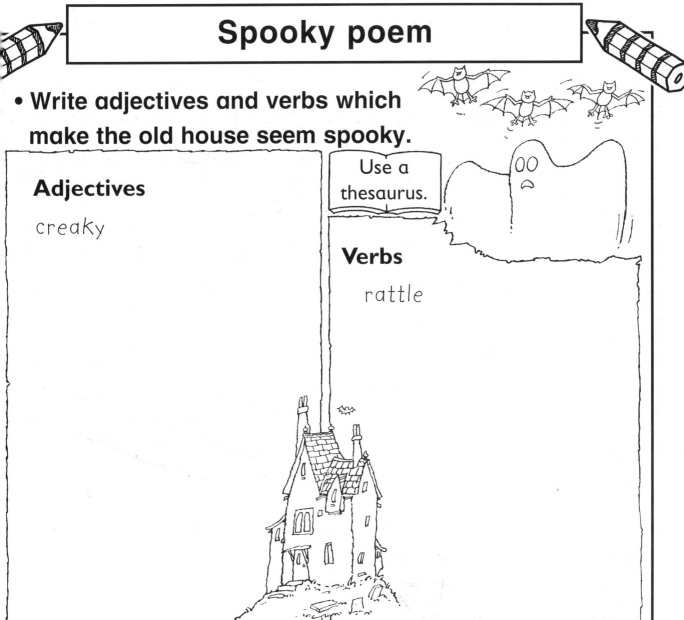

Adjectives

creaky

Use a thesaurus.

Verbs

rattle

- **Arrange the adjectives and verbs to make a spooky poem.**

Now try this!

Your poem doesn't have to rhyme.

_____

_____

_____

_____

_____

_____

Teachers' note Before the children begin this activity they should have had the opportunity to read 'spooky' poems (see **Notes on the activities**, pages 7–8). Ask them to suggest 'spooky' words to describe the old house and to suggest 'spooky' things which might happen there. Encourage the children who tackle the extension activity to type out their spooky poems for display.

Developing Literacy Poetry Compendium: Ages 7–11 © A & C BLACK

On and on

- **Read the poem.**
- **Underline the** repeated words .
- **What goes on for ever?**

  _____

- **Which three things change?**

  _____

  _____

  _____

- **List other things which might change, or come and go.**

Sea Timeless Song

Hurricane come
and hurricane go
but sea – sea timeless

sea timeless
sea timeless
sea timeless
sea timeless

Hibiscus bloom
then dry-wither so
but sea – sea timeless

sea timeless
sea timeless
sea timeless
sea timeless

Tourist come
and tourist go
but sea – sea timeless

sea timeless
sea timeless
sea timeless
sea timeless

Grace Nichols

Now try this!

- **Write another verse for the poem.**

  _____

  _____

  _____

  _____

  _____

  _____

Remember the repeated lines.

Teachers' note Ask the children what they notice about the rhythm of the repeated lines and why the poet has repeated them. They should notice that they have the rhythm of waves washing in and out on the shore. Discuss the things in the poem which change and the things which do not. The children could go on to make up a class 'Sea Timeless Song'.

**Developing Literacy
Poetry Compendium:
Ages 7–11
© A & C BLACK**

Day and night

- **What is the poem about?**

  _____

- **How could you change it to a poem about nightfall?**

- **Underline the words you would change.**

- **On the notepad write words you could use instead.**

The World is Day-Breaking

The world is day-breaking!
The world is day-breaking!

Day arises
From its sleep.
Day wakes up
With the dawning light.
The world is day-breaking!
The world is day-breaking!

Anonymous

Opposites might be useful.

Use a dictionary.

Use a thesaurus.

Now try this!

- **Use your notes to help you to write a poem about nightfall.**

  The world is _____

  _____

  _____

  _____

  _____

  _____

  _____

Teachers' note Ask the children what they notice about the pattern of the poem. They should notice the repeated lines and their effect – of a gradual awakening, rather like someone opening his or her eyes, yawning and stretching.

Developing Literacy Poetry Compendium: Ages 7–11 © A & C BLACK

Travel rhymes

- **Read the first rhyme.**
- **Fill in the gaps with verbs that** rhyme **with the places.**

Find a picture that gives you a clue.

- **Write place names to rhyme with the verbs.**

Use an atlas.

NOW try this!

Walk to
_____

Dance to
_____

Fly to
_____

Tear to
_____

- **Write four others.**

Teachers' note Read the first two examples with the children and ask them to suggest rhyming verbs for the next two or three. The verbs should all be in some way linked with travelling. For the extension activity provide atlases, including United Kingdom road atlases which list even the smallest villages.

Developing Literacy
Poetry Compendium:
Ages 7–11
© A & C BLACK

Monday's child

• **Read the poem.**

Monday's child is fair of face,
Tuesday's child is full of grace,
Wednesday's child is full of woe,
Thursday's child has far to go,
Friday's child is loving and giving,
Saturday's child works hard for a living,
But the child who is born on the Sabbath day
Is bonny and blithe and good and gay.

Anonymous

• **Use the rhyme-finder to help you to write other words**
  for the poem.

Rhyme-finder			You could add other words to the rhyme-finder.
dear	deed	care	
fear	need	share	
live	heart	kind	
give	part	mind	
sadness	brothers	healthy	caring
gladness	others	wealthy	daring

Monday's child is *always healthy*

Tuesday's child is _____

Wednesday's child is _____

_____

_____

_____

Teachers' note Ask the children to read the poem aloud and to notice, and maybe circle, the pairs of rhyming words before thinking up alternative lines for the poem. Point out that their new poem must follow the time sequence of the original. The children could use a computer to draft and edit their own version.

Developing Literacy
Poetry Compendium:
Ages 7–11
© A & C BLACK

Heavy or light

- **Say the words in the box. Listen to their sounds.**
- **Write the words in the correct bags.**

air	dread	knob	peep
barge	fall	leap	ping
blip	flab	lump	plod
clang	glee	may	rubble
clod	hip	mud	sail
dip	ice	mug	waddle

The heavy gang

barge

The light brigade

air

Now try this!

- **Write four more words in each bag.**
- **Write four lines for a heavy or light poem.**

The lines don't have to rhyme.

Teachers' note With the children, read some of the words in the box aloud and ask them to listen to the sound of each word and to say 'heavy' or 'light' after each one. Other heavy-sounding words include clomp, clump, flog, slog and slump; other light-sounding words include fairy, sing, sip, sky and tip.

Developing Literacy
Poetry Compendium:
Ages 7–11
© A & C BLACK

Alliterative allsorts

- **Fill in the missing words so that they have** alliteration .

> Alliteration is when words start with the same sound.

Examples:

a piece of pie

a jar of jam

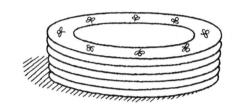

a pile of plates

They must make sense.

Example: a vase of violets **but not** a vase of vests

a bunch of _____

a bottle of _____

a hunk of _____

a dish of _____

a chunk of _____

a cup of _____

a lump of _____

a basket of _____

a mug of _____

a slice of _____

a bowl of _____

a litre of _____

a pan of _____

a plate of _____

a tray of _____

a can of _____

Now try this!

- **List other containers or parts of things.**
- **Think of things to go with them. They must start with the same** sound .

Teachers' note Read a list of alliterative parts or containers and contents and ask the children what they notice about the words: for example, a pile of paper, a heap of hay, a box of biscuits, a spoonful of sugar and a portion of paella.

Developing Literacy Poetry Compendium: Ages 7–11
© A & C BLACK

Still as a post and tall as a spire

Poets sometimes use comparisons to describe things.

• **Match the comparisons to the pictures.**

tall as a spire	necks like rods	snug as a nest

lonely as a cloud	broad as a barn door	teeth like splinters

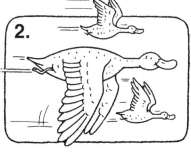

Picture	Comparison
1	lonely as a cloud

Now try this!

• **Write comparisons for these.**

...an old tree

...a flamingo standing still

...a strong gust of wind

...a cat rushing across a garden

...a scruffy child

...a noisy, clanking, old car.

Use the words like or as.

Teachers' note Revise similes and introduce comparisons which use 'like' rather than 'as'. The children could consider the different impressions created by comparisons: for example, 'whistled like a kettle', 'whistled like the wind', 'long fingers like snakes', 'long fingers like twigs'.

Developing Literacy Poetry Compendium: Ages 7–11
© A & C BLACK

Comparisons

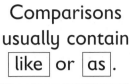

Comparisons usually contain like or as.

When you say something is like something else, you are making a comparison.

as dry as a bone

as light as a feather

• **Underline the comparisons in this poem.**

How to Make a Greyhound

It needs
A head like a snake, a neck like a drake,
A back like a beam, a belly like a bream,
A foot like a cat, and a tail like a rat.

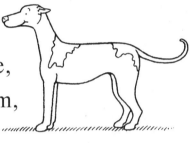

Anonymous

• **Complete this poem about how to make a butterfly.**

It needs
Wings like ⎯⎯⎯⎯⎯⎯⎯⎯⎯⎯⎯⎯⎯,
Feelers like ⎯⎯⎯⎯⎯⎯⎯⎯⎯⎯⎯,
Eyes like ⎯⎯⎯⎯⎯⎯⎯⎯⎯⎯⎯⎯,
A body like a ⎯⎯⎯⎯⎯⎯⎯⎯⎯⎯,
And a sound like ⎯⎯⎯⎯⎯⎯⎯⎯⎯.

NOW try this!

• **Write another 'how to make an animal' poem.**

Use comparisons.

Teachers' note Introduce the activity by asking the children to complete comparisons such as 'tall like a...', 'as smooth as ...', 'winding like a ...', 'as soft as...', 'as gentle as ...', 'grey like ...'. They could use comparisons to describe things in the classroom. Ask the others to guess what is being described, or display the descriptions for others to solve later.

Developing Literacy Poetry Compendium: Ages 7–11 © A & C BLACK

The same but different: 1

1.

Cats

Cats sleep
Anywhere,
Any table,
Any chair,
Top of piano,
Window-ledge,
In the middle,
On the edge,
Open drawer,
Empty shoe,
Anybody's
Lap will do,
Fitted in a
Cardboard box,
In the cupboard
With your frocks –
Anywhere!
They don't care!
Cats sleep
Anywhere.

Eleanor Farjeon

2.

At midnight in the alley
    A Tom-cat comes to wail,
And he chants the hate of a million years
    As he swings his snaky tail...

He will lie on a rug tomorrow
    And lick his silky fur,
And veil the brute in his yellow eyes
    And play he's tame, and purr.

But at midnight in the alley
    He will crouch again and wail,
And beat the time for his demon's song
    With a swing of his demon's tail.

From *The Tom-Cat* by Don Marquis

Teachers' note Before the activity, allocate one of the poems to each group of children, so that half the class reads one poem and half the other; give them time to discuss and decide how the poem should be read aloud and invite them to read it while the others listen. Continued on page 25.

Developing Literacy
Poetry Compendium:
Ages 7–11
© A & C BLACK

• **What do the two poems tell you?**

• **Complete the chart.**

	✔ or ✗		Words or phrases which tell me this	
	1	2	Poem 1	Poem 2
The poet has watched cats sleeping.				
The poet has watched a cat outdoors.				
Cats do not take much notice of people.				
Cats pretend to like people.				
Cats are evil.				
Cats are awake at night.				
Cats sleep a lot.				
Cats do not need a special place to sleep in.				
Cats have soft fur.				

Now try this!

• **Is either poem a good advert for cats? Why?**

Teachers' note Use this with page 24. It provides a framework on which the children can organise their opinions and helps them to explain the different views the two poets have of the same subject.

Developing Literacy
Poetry Compendium:
Ages 7–11
© A & C BLACK

Catch the hatchet!

- **Take turns with a partner to fill in the gaps with** [tch] **words.**

The words in each shape form a line of the poem.

Catch the hatchet!

Snatch it!

Watch it!

- **Read the poem you have made.**
- **Does it sound fast or slow?** _____

Now try this!

- **List some words which have a smooth sound.**
- **Use some of them to write a poem with a slow movement.**

follow, calling, valley ...

Teachers' note Discuss the quick, jerky effect of a series of 'tch' words. The children could first try this activity orally, taking turns to add a 'tch' word (the words should have the 'tch' sound, but their spellings need not include the letter string: for example, rich, such and much). Ask them to explain the reasoning behind their choice of words.

Developing Literacy Poetry Compendium: Ages 7–11 © A & C BLACK

Onomatopoeia collections

Words which have `onomatopoeia` **really sound like their meanings.**

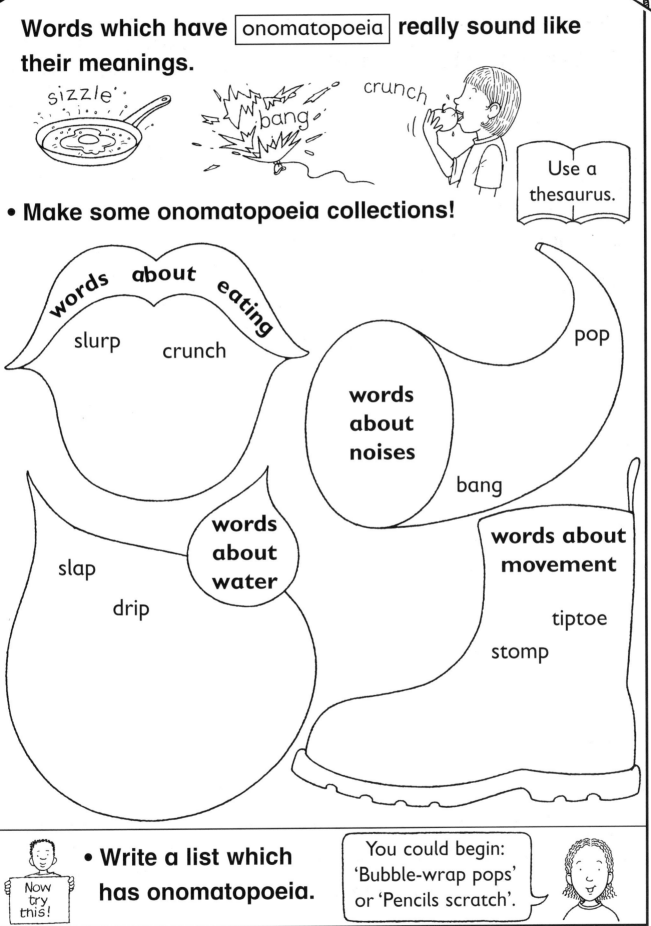

sizzle

bang

crunch

Use a thesaurus.

• **Make some onomatopoeia collections!**

words about eating

slurp

crunch

pop

words about noises

bang

words about water

slap

drip

words about movement

tiptoe

stomp

Now try this!

• **Write a list which has onomatopoeia.**

You could begin: 'Bubble-wrap pops' or 'Pencils scratch'.

Teachers' note Read out a list of words with onomatopoeia and ask the children what they notice about the sounds of the words: for example, animal sounds such as moo, quack, roar and squeak. In the extension activity the children should write a list which is relevant to a particular place or topic: for example, the classroom, or an appliance such as a washing machine.

Developing Literacy Poetry Compendium: Ages 7–11 © A & C BLACK

Splash poem

• **Write all the words you can think of about rain.**

Use a thesaurus.

Write nouns, verbs and adjectives.

slop
puddle
shiny

• **Use some of the words to write a poem about rain. Write a word or phrase on each splash and puddle.**

Now try this!

Teachers' note Introduce the activity by reading shape poems with the children (see **Notes on the activities**, page 9). During the introductory session provide a bowl of water and invite the children to splash the water around. Ask them to suggest words to describe what they see, hear and feel.

Developing Literacy
Poetry Compendium:
Ages 7–11
© A & C BLACK

Shape sentences

• **Complete the shape sentences.**

The snake slithered

Leaves

dropped

Snowflakes

Up the ladder

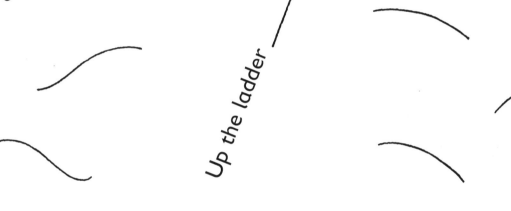

The silent snail

A thumb

and

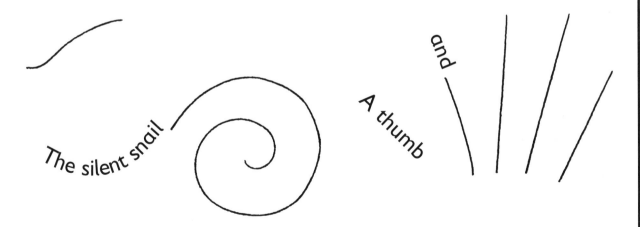

Now try this!

• **Write shape sentences about these.**

| a fish | a spider | a star |

Teachers' note Introduce the activity by inviting the children to suggest ways in which to complete the first sentence and to explain their choice of words. Record their responses and discuss ways in which they can be refined and improved before choosing the most effective. Encourage the children to approach the other examples in the same way.

Developing Literacy
Poetry Compendium:
Ages 7–11
© A & C BLACK

Word shapes

• Write the words which are hidden in the shapes.

```
      d
    i a
  m o n
d d i a m
o n d d i a m
o n d d i a
m o n d d
  i a m
    o n
      d
```

```
      d
    r o p
  o f w a t
e r d r o p o
f w a t e r d r
o p o f w a t e r
d r o p o f w a t
e r d r o p o f w
  a t e r d r o
    p o f w a
      t e r
```

```
        s
      t a
    r f i s h
s t a r f i s h s t a r
  f i s h s t a r
    f i s h s t a
  r f i        s h s
  t a              r i h
  f
s                    h
```

_____

```
      i
    c e c
  r e a m c
o n e i c e
c r e a m c o
n e i c e c r e a
m c o n e i c
e c r e a m
  c o n e i
    c e c r
    e a m
    c o n
      e
```

```
        p
      o t o f
    t e a p o t o
    f t e a p o t o
  t e a p o t o f t e a      f
  o t o f t e a p o t o        p
    t e a p o t o f t          e
    a p o t o f t e        a
      p o t o f
        t e a
```

```
        s t i c k
    y l o l l i p o p s
    t i c k y l o l l i p
  o p s t i c k y l o l l i
  p o p s t i c k y l o l l
    i p o p s t i c k y l o
    l l i p o p s t i c k
      y l o l l i p o p
        s t i c
              y
              l
              o
              l
              l
              i
              p
              o
              p
```

_____

```
    s t e g o
  s a u r u s s t e
    g o s a u r u s s t e g
      o s a u r u s s t e g o s a
  u r u s s t e g o s a u r u s s t e g o
    s a u r u s s t e g o s a u r u s s t e
      g o s a u r u s s t e g o s a u r
      u s t e g o s a u r u s
```

_____

Now try this!

• Write word shapes for these.

| a pair of jeans | a blue balloon |

Teachers' note The children could make their own word shapes by drawing an outline using a heavy line, and placing it underneath the paper on which they are going to write the words.

Developing Literacy Poetry Compendium: Ages 7–11
© A & C BLACK

Calligrams

Calligrams are words shaped like their meanings.

- **Write calligrams in the boxes.**

crack

Kick

break	fly

scary

wobbling

short

touching down

tall

taking off

 Now try this!

- **Write calligrams for these.**

explosion   music   slide

Teachers' note Before the lesson, collect and display examples of calligrams from advertisements and enlarge and display calligrams from poetry books. Encourage the children to try out on scrap paper the different ways in which they could write the nouns and verbs they find in a dictionary or thesaurus.

Developing Literacy
Poetry Compendium:
Ages 7–11
© A & C BLACK

Ptarmigans and pterodactyls

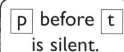

• **Read the poem aloud.**

| p | before | t |
is silent.

The ptarmigan is strange
As strange as strange can be;
Never sits on ptelephone poles
Or roosts upon a ptree.
And the way he ptakes to spelling
Is the strangest thing to me.

Anonymous

• **Change these to 'ptarmigan' words.**

tail __ptail__   talk _____   tall _____

talons _____   tame _____   tap _____

tell _____   temper _____   ten _____

• **Make up six other 'ptarmigan' words.**

_____   _____   _____

_____   _____   _____

Now try this!

• **Make up a poem about a pterodactyl.**
• **Use the ptarmigan poem as a model.**

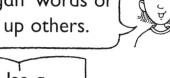

Use your 'ptarmigan' words or make up others.

Use a dictionary.

Teachers' note Introduce the silent 'p' (for example, in 'psalm'). Revise silent letters such as the silent 'k' in 'knife' and the silent 'b' in 'bomb'. The children could use a dictionary to find words beginning with 't' to which they can add a silent initial 'p'. They could also play word games using the silent 'p'.

Developing Literacy Poetry Compendium: Ages 7–11
© A & C BLACK

Word jokes

• **Write the answers to these jokes.**

Clue
Look for pairs of words whose first sounds can be swapped.

What's the difference between...

...a forged ten pound note and a crazy rabbit?

One's bad money; the other's a

_____.

...a worker's hat and a door for a pet?

One's a flat cap; the other's a

_____.

...part of Australia and a chilly ghoul?

One's the Gold Coast; the other's a

_____.

...being greedy and grilling bread?

One's taking most; the other's

_____.

Now try this!

• **Write jokes about these.**

| a cracked pane and a packed crane |

| a tie pin and a pie tin |

| a long road and a wrong load |

Teachers' note To introduce the activity write pairs of words on a large piece of paper. Cover the beginnings of the words with paper and invite the children to exchange the beginning of one word with that of another. They could also write and illustrate 'word-pair jokes' of their own for a partner to guess the answers.

Developing Literacy
Poetry Compendium:
Ages 7–11
© A & C BLACK

33

Absurd words

- ## Complete the 'absurd word' captions.

the sea bed

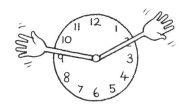

the hands of
a clock

the bonnet of

_____

a car

_____

a disc

_____

a daffodil

_____

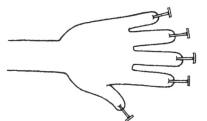

finger

_____

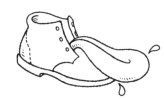

the tongue of

_____

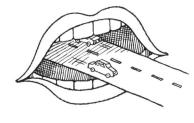

_____

of a tunnel

_____

of a building

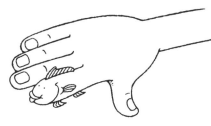

_____

_____ finger

Now try this!

- ## Draw and write captions for four other 'absurd words'.

Teachers' note During the introductory session, discuss words the children know which have more than one meaning: for example, bridge, crook, eye, foot, head, leaf. Ask the children to explain the first two examples, then model the third and fourth and ask them to explain those, too. They could discuss the rest with a partner before completing the activity.

Developing Literacy
Poetry Compendium:
Ages 7–11
© A & C BLACK

Legs riddle

- **Work out the meaning of the** `riddle`**.**
- **What are:**

  two legs? _____

  three legs? _____

  four legs? _____

  one leg? _____

Two legs sat upon three legs
With one leg in a bag;
In comes four legs
And runs away with one leg;
Up jumps two legs,
Catches up three legs,
Throws it after four legs,
And makes him bring back
       one leg.
         Anonymous

- **Tell the story of the riddle.**

Lines 1 and 2

Lines 3 and 4

Lines 5 and 6

Lines 7 and 8

NOW try this!

- **Write a 'wheels' riddle.**

First write lists of things with one or more wheels.

Teachers' note Introduce the activity with short and simple riddles about items in the classroom: for example, 'a sheaf of white leaves with black markings' (an exercise book), 'the more you use it the shorter it becomes' (chalk or a pencil). In the extension activity the children could include a wheelbarrow, a unicycle, a bicycle, a tricycle, a car, a bus, a truck and so on.

Developing Literacy
Poetry Compendium:
Ages 7–11
© A & C BLACK

Twister

- **Read the** tongue-twister **aloud.**

Use a dictionary.

Theophilus Thistledown, the successful thistle sifter,
In sifting a sieve of unsifted thistles,
Thrust three thousand unsifted thistles
Through the thick of his thumb.

Anonymous

- **Which two** phonemes **twist the tongue in the poem?**

- **Make two lists of words which contain these two phonemes.**

The phonemes can have different spellings.

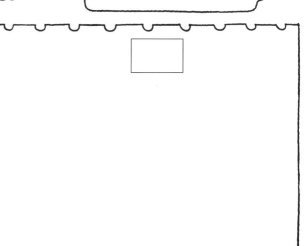

- **Make up a tongue-twister using some of the words you have listed.**

Now try this!

Tongue-twisters can be silly!

_____

_____

_____

_____

Teachers' note Read the tongue-twister and ask the children to have a try. Ask them which two phonemes are repeated. They could think of other pairs of phonemes which make words difficult to read quickly: for example 'w' and 'r' and 'gr' and 'g'. Encourage the children who tackle the extension activity to word-process their tongue-twisters for display.

Developing Literacy Poetry Compendium: Ages 7–11 © A & C BLACK

Notes on the activities

The notes below expand upon those provided at the bottom of the activity pages. They give ideas and suggestions for making the most of the activity sheet, including suggestions for the whole-class introduction, the plenary session or for follow-up work using an adapted version of the sheet. To help teachers to select appropriate learning experiences for their pupils, the activities are grouped into units in line with the Primary Framework for Literacy, but the pages need not be presented in the order in which they appear, unless stated otherwise.

Unit 1: Creating images

Some of the poems in this section include words which will be new to the children, but which they can enjoy for their sounds even before they know what they mean. The activities develop their understanding of rhyme, rhythm, the effects of the sounds of words and figurative language such as similes and their appreciation of how poets create effects through these devices. There are opportunities for using ICT to create images: computer software, audio recordings and video/DVD recordings.

Everyday rhythms (page 41). This activity introduces the idea of the effects of words by drawing the children's attention to the rhythms they hear all around them, developing their ability to 'hear' words in everyday rhythms (many children do this spontaneously).

Sing a song of people and **A film of the poem** (pages 42–43). Encourage the children to visualise the scene and rhythmic events of the poem – the images created by the poet's words. For the introductory scene of their film, some children might want to go straight into the action, while others might prefer to show a still picture of a city street with images of people made from card glued onto lolly sticks, and then suddenly make the people start to move about as they begin reading the poem. For the ending, some children might choose to stop suddenly, while others might prefer to show just one person watching as the fast-moving people leave the set. The pictures could be created during subsequent art or ICT lessons (during which further, practical, planning might be needed). The tableaux could even be filmed. To create animated images of the movement of people in the poem the children could cut out pictures of people in action from magazines and newspapers and show them one after the other in different positions on the computer screen. Let them experiment with the effects and ask them to test them while reading the poem aloud. They could also create city scenes for a still background from newspaper pictures. The American expressions 'subway', 'elevator' and 'sidewalk' could be discussed (ask the children what they are called in Britain). This could be linked with sentence structure work on standard English and different forms of English. Page 43 could also be used with other fairly long poems which have a noticeable rhythm and plenty of action (slow or fast): for example, 'A Visit from St Nicholas' (Clement Clarke Moore) and 'The Car Trip' (Michael Rosen) in *The Hutchinson Treasury of Children's Poetry*, or poems chosen by the children themselves.

Three ships (page 44). This poem looks more difficult than it is! The children can gain an impression of each of the three ships (the quinquireme, the galleon and the coaster) by considering the meanings of the  words they know and by listening to the sounds of the unfamiliar words. Discuss the sounds of the words: for example, 'butted' sounds dull, heavy and rough, whereas 'rowing' and 'dipping' sound light and graceful.

Lively language (page 45). This activity enlarges the children's vocabulary of interesting adjectives and verbs and encourages them to think of alternatives to use in their writing. You could link it with sentence structure work on verbs and adjectives.

Make an impression (page 46). This page shows the ways in which poets choose words to create an impression using figures of speech. Figurative language can include similes (see pages 47–48) which create ideas about something by reminding the reader of something else. The extracts are from 'The Tom-Cat' by Don Marquis; 'The Eagle' and 'Today I Saw a Dragon-Fly' by Alfred, Lord Tennyson; 'Timothy Winters' by Charles Causley; 'Preludes' by T. S. Eliot and 'Daffodils' by William Wordsworth. They are all in *The Puffin Book of Classic Verse*.

Simile stars and **A simile poem** (pages 47–48). Encourage the children to notice fresh similes which poets themselves have made up rather than using the common ones, which have become clichés (for example, 'as dead as a doornail'), and to make up some of their own. In **A simile poem** they can have fun writing about how brilliant they are (or would like to be). They learn how poets use language to create a vivid picture in words.

A poem from the past (page 49). This develops the children's understanding of the ways in which language and the conventions of poetry have changed over time. *Main activity answers*: goes – goeth, does not stumble – stumbles not, calmly – stilly, seizes – seizeth, chosen – appointed, feeds – doth feed, does – doth, it is – 'tis. *Extension activity answers*: goes, goeth, stumbles, do, 's, may endure, do…go, makes, seizeth, doth feed, range, gare, find, doth…go, ('t)is, do travel, aim, do procure. Some of the verbs have unusual forms: they end in 'eth' instead of 's' (for example, 'goeth'). Others are no longer used (for example, 'gare').

Rhyme choice (page 50). This is a cloze exercise which requires the children to read carefully the poem 'Windy Nights' by Robert Louis Stevenson so that they understand it well enough to select the most appropriate words with which to fill the gaps. It develops skills in using syntax and context when reading for meaning. The children need to consider both the sense of the poem and its rhyme pattern. *Answers*: wet, by, about, sea, loud, he, again.

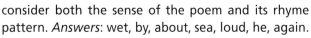

Fantastic football (page 51). Encourage the children to try out ideas for alliteration – to enjoy the sounds of words.

A skylark sang (page 52). This activity develops the children's appreciation of the ways in which a poet uses alliteration to create effects: the soaring, singing effect of the repeated 's' sounds in the first three verses and the long, lingering sounds of the repeated 'l' sounds in verse 4.

Morning and **Night** (pages 53–54). These pages are based on a poem related to a familiar experience, about which the children can comment; they can compare the morning of the poem with their own mornings and write their own 'night' poems using 'Morning' as a model.

School poem (page 55). This poem is about experiences familiar to the children. It explores the meanings of words and encourages the children to have fun with them. Discuss the way in which a poet uses the meanings as well as the sounds of words to create images and humour.

Write a mystery poem (page 56). The children could also use this for planning other types of poem: blank out and alter the relevant words. It helps them to think about a scene, picture it and think about the sounds and how it might feel there before going on to consider the words that will best create this image. After they have listed the words, encourage the children to read them aloud, combine them to describe the scene and think about the effects they create. They could discuss this with a partner and select the words that best produce the effect they want.

Unit 2: Exploring form

This section introduces some of the forms in which poems can be written and provides structures to help the children to write poems using the forms of those they have read as models. Before beginning these activities the children should have had opportunities to count the syllables in words and then in lines of poetry.

Haiku (page 57). This activity models the process of writing a haiku. Read several haiku with the children before they begin this page, so that they can appreciate their style. Ask them what kinds of subject haiku are about. For more information about haiku and more examples, see *The Iron Book of British Haiku* (David Cobb & Martin Lucas, Iron Press, 1998). The writing of haiku originated in medieval Japan and tried to capture the 'essence' of its subject, which is usually some aspect of the natural world. The seventeen syllables of a haiku are arranged in three lines: five, seven, five. Often the last line adds an element of surprise or contrast.

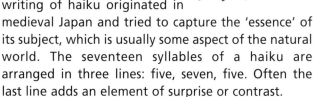

Writing a tanka (page 58). In this activity a structure is provided to help the children to write notes for, and then compose, a tanka. Tanka, like haiku, originated in Japan: people would send haiku to one another and sometimes reply by adding two lines, thus forming a tanka. Examples of tanka can be found in many children's anthologies, including *The Works* (Macmillan, 2000).

Cinquain consequences (page 59). This introduces the format of the cinquain, which is thought to have been devised by the American poet Adelaide Crapsey (1870–1914): for example, the following, written in 1913:

November Nights
Listen…
With faint dry sound
Like steps of passing ghosts,
the leaves, frost-crisp'd, break from the trees
And fall.

A cinquain can be described using the comparison 'like an elastic band stretched to its limit – and then snapping back again'. Other cinquains can be found in *The Works* (Macmillan, 2000).

List poems (page 60). Here the children meet a simple example of the type of list poem which they could write for themselves. To help them you could provide train timetables or let the children look them up on the Internet (key in 'train timetables' on the search engine or look at maps of rail routes). Read the poem aloud while the children listen, then repeat it and invite them to join in. Ask them what the rhythm reminds them of and what the poem is about. They should notice that the names of the stations have been arranged to give a train-like rhythm.

A 'thin' poem (page 61). This is an example of a 'thin' poem, about a dandelion clock, which has the rhythm of a ticking clock. The children could speak the poem as a group, with half the group saying the words while the others (quietly) repeat 'tick-tock'. Give them time to plan this and encourage them to make sure that everyone in the group has a say. They could experiment with the effects of layout. Let them key in the poem and rearrange the text: for example, in short and then long lines or as sentences. Ask them how this affects the way in which they read it and demonstrate that the length of the lines, as well as the words themselves, creates the clock rhythm.

Alphabetical haunted castle (page 62). The alphabetical poem has a familiar format; it can be linked with work on alliteration. Ask the children to read their poems aloud while the others listen and make a note of the most effective words and phrases. Invite feedback, including why they think these words or phrases are effective. Draw their attention to the sounds of the words. They could also write alphabetical poems to help younger children to learn the alphabet.

A conversation poem (page 63). This is based on a traditional poem which is likely to be familiar to the children. Provide copies of the complete poem for the children to read before the lesson. You can  find it in *The Oxford Nursery Rhyme Book* (Peter & Hilda Opie, OUP) and on several websites including: www.rhymes.org.uk, www.love-poems.me.uk and www.landofnurseryrhymes.co.uk.

A monologue and **Prayers: 1** and **2** (pages 64–66). In these activities the children are required to consider the formats and purposes of monologues and prayers. These prepare for sentence structure work on the first, second and third person, and can also be linked with work in religious education. Explain Martin Luther King's 'Dream' (his mission to gain civil rights for black people). The children might need to be told that the Iroquois are Native Americans. As an introduction to the activities it will be useful to talk about the children's experiences of prayers: to whom they are speaking if they say a prayer and what prayers are for.

Epitaphs (page 67). This page presents a collection of serious and humorous epitaphs: 1) is of unknown origin, 2) is of unknown origin, 3) is from *Epitaph on a Hare* by William Cowper, 4) is of unknown origin, 5) is about Charles II (1630–85) written by John Wilmot, Earl of Rochester, and 6) is from *Epitaph on a Child* by Robert Herrick. Explain that, although it is a sad time when someone dies, many people do not want their friends and family to be sad when they die; they may even write their own humorous epitaphs.

Learning objectives

The following chart shows how the Ages 8–9 activity sheets (pages 41–67) match the learning objectives addressed by the Year 4 units in the Poetry block of the Primary Framework for Literacy. (Where a page number is shown in bold type, this indicates the learning objective is the main focus of the activity.)

Objectives	Unit 1: Creating images	Unit 2: Exploring form
Speaking		
Respond appropriately on the contributions of others in light of differing viewpoints	42, 50, 53, 54	59, 63, 65, 66
Word structure and spelling		
Use knowledge of phonics, morphology and etymology to spell new and unfamiliar words	51, 54, 56	59–63
Understanding and interpreting texts		
Explain how writers use figurative and expressive language to create images and atmosphere	**41, 44, 46, 47, 50, 51, 52, 53, 54**	57, 60, **62**, 65, 66
Engaging with and responding to texts		
Read extensively favourite authors/genres and experiment with other types of text	42, 45, 48	57–59, **60**, 61, 62, **63**, 64, **65, 66**, 67
Interrogate texts to deepen and clarify understanding and response	**42**, 44, 46, **48, 49**, 50, 52, **55**	57–59, 61, **64**, 66, **67**
Explore why and how writers write, including through face-to-face and online contact with authors	48, 49, 52, 53, 55	57, 61, 67
Creating and shaping texts		
Develop and refine ideas in writing using planning and problem-solving strategies	43, 45, 54, **56**	57, **58**, 59, 60, **61**, 62, 63
Choose and combine words, images and other features for particular effects	41, **43, 45**, 47, 48, 50, 51, 54, 56	**57**, 58, **59**, 61
Presentation		
Write consistently with neat, legible and joined handwriting	41, 43, 45–56	57–64, 66, 67
Use word-processing packages to present written work and continue to increase speed and accuracy in typing	44, 48, 54	61

Everyday rhythms

You can experiment with words to create rhythms.

Example: the rhythm of a ticking clock

teacup, teacup, teacup,
teacup, teacup, teacup.

Use one or more words for a rhythm.

- **Choose words from the word-bank to create these rhythms.**

		Word-bank
windscreen wipers		arm
a heartbeat		bee
a pelican crossing bleeper		cricket
a stapler		crumble
a police siren		crumple
a washing machine		dumb-bell
		double
		far
		knee
		near
		out
		pea
		ticket
		washing
		wishing
		wristwatch

Now try this!

- **Write word-rhythms for four other everyday things.**

Teachers' note Take the children for a walk during which they are likely to hear different rhythmic sounds, such as pelican crossings, road drills, hammers and cars, and encourage them to listen to rhythmic sounds in the school: printers, staplers and fans. Can they 'hear' words in the sounds? The children could also write a 'word-rhythm' poem.

Developing Literacy
Poetry Compendium:
Ages 7–11
© A & C BLACK

Sing a song of people

Sing a Song of People

Sing a song of people
Walking fast or slow;
People in the city
Up and down they go.

People on the sidewalk,
People on the bus;
People passing, passing,
In back and front of us.
People on the subway
Underneath the ground;
People riding taxis
Round and round and round.

People with their hats on,
Going in the doors;
People with umbrellas
When it rains and pours.
People in tall buildings
And in the stores below;
Riding elevators
Up and down they go.

People walking singly,
People in a crowd;
People saying nothing,
People talking loud.
People laughing, smiling,
Grumpy people too;
People who just hurry
And never look at you!

Sing a song of people
Who like to come and go;
Song of city people
You see but never know!

Lois Lenski

Teachers' note See also page 43. Read the poem aloud and ask the children to describe what they 'see': the setting, the objects and people. Encourage the children to be specific: for example, if they say that people in the poem are moving quickly, ask them what the people are doing – running, walking quickly, dashing or darting about?

**Developing Literacy
Poetry Compendium:
Ages 7–11
© A & C BLACK**

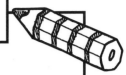

A film of the poem

- **Make notes to plan a film of the poem 'Sing a Song of People'.**

Title

Setting

Introduction

| **Background** | **The scene** | **Actions** |

List and describe objects in the background.

Describe what is happening. Use powerful verbs.

Ending

What will you see as the film ends?

Teachers' note Use this with page 42. The children should notice the fast pace of the poem and the 'dashing', 'darting about' rhythm of people constantly on the move.

Developing Literacy
Poetry Compendium:
Ages 7–11
© A & C BLACK

Three ships

- **Read the poem aloud.**

  Listen to the sounds and

  rhythms of the words.

Cargoes

Quinquireme of Nineveh from distant Ophir
Rowing home to haven in sunny Palestine,
With a cargo of ivory,
And apes and peacocks,
Sandalwood, cedarwood, and sweet white wine.

Stately Spanish galleon coming from the Isthmus,
Dipping through the Tropics by the palm-green shores,
With a cargo of diamonds,
Emeralds, amethysts,
Topazes, and cinnamon, and gold moidores.

Dirty British coaster with salt-caked smoke-stack
Butting through the Channel in the mad March days,
With a cargo of Tyne coal,
Road-rail, pig-lead,
Firewood, ironware, and cheap tin trays.

John Masefield

Glossary

Isthmus the Isthmus of Panama, a narrow strip of land between North and South America
moidores (moydors) Portuguese gold coins
Nineveh (*nin*nevuh) the ancient capital of Assyria, now part of Iraq
Ophir (oh*feer*) an ancient area thought to have been somewhere in India
quinquireme (*kwin*kwi*reem*) a large ship rowed by five banks of oars, one above the other

- **Which adjectives in the word-bank describe each ship?**
- **Make a chart to record the adjectives.**

First ship	Second ship	Third ship

Word-bank

bright
colourful
dirty
dull
elegant
glamorous
graceful
grand
grimy
ordinary
plain
rich
rough
unusual

Now try this!

- **List the words you would use to write about a boat or ship you have seen.**

Teachers' note Read the poem aloud and then invite the children to practise the pronunciation and rhythm of the difficult words before they join in a reading. What impression do they have of each ship even before they find out the meanings of the unusual words? They could draw their impressions. Show them how to word-process a chart or table for this activity.

Developing Literacy
Poetry Compendium:
Ages 7–11
© A & C BLACK

44

Lively language

- **Choose adjectives and verbs from the word-bank for each building.**

Word-bank

Adjectives
aging
cosy
decaying
dingy
grand
homely
quaint
rotting
simple
snug
solid
spanking new
sparkling
spick and span
stately

Verbs
crouches
looms
nestles
perches
poses
rattles
rests
rises
shivers
soars

A castle

A cottage

An old shed

A new detached house

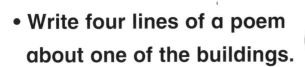

- **Write four lines of a poem about one of the buildings.**

The lines don't have to rhyme.

Teachers' note It may be necessary to revise adjectives and verbs. Discuss the different impressions created by different adjectives and verbs with similar meanings: for example, 'stately doorway'/'grand doorway'/'big doorway', 'towers' or 'nestles' instead of 'stands' or 'is'. Model some examples with the children and encourage them to use a thesaurus.

Developing Literacy
Poetry Compendium:
Ages 7–11
© A & C BLACK

45

Make an impression

Poets use | figurative language | **to create impressions.**

Example:

'... the blotched red moon leers over the roofs'

This is about the Moon, but it gives the impression of a person looking in an unpleasant way.

- **What are these examples about?**
- **What impressions do they give?**

The wrinkled sea beneath him crawls

A living flash of light he flew

His hair is an exclamation mark.

The burnt-out ends of smoky days.

Tossing their heads in sprightly dance

Now try this!

- **Make notes of words you could use in a poem about the Sun. Use figurative language.**

Think of words which give impressions of brightness, heat, a source of energy...

Teachers' note Read one of the poems in its entirety to the children (see **Notes on the activities**, page 37) and ask them what impression the poet is trying to give of the subject. Discuss the different impressions which can be created by figurative language used to describe the same thing: for example, 'He clasps the crag'/'he perches on a rock'/'he clings to a ledge'.

Developing Literacy
Poetry Compendium:
Ages 7–11
© A & C BLACK

Simile stars

Poets use similes to compare things.

Different similes give different impressions.

Examples: falls like a drifting leaf

falls like a heavy stone

- **Complete the similes on the rockets.**

Use words from the stars.

singing bird

nib

petals

sweet peas like _____

scattery as _____

threw words like _____

bright butterflies

eyelashes

snake

lighter than _____

My heart is like a _____ whose nest is in a watered shoot

as sharp as a _____

as tricky as a ten-foot

stones

- **Write six other similes.**
- **Label each simile to say what it is about.**

Now try this!

Avoid common similes like 'as light as a feather'.

Teachers' note Revise the common similes the children have come across: for example, 'as bold as brass', 'as hard as iron' and so on, and ask them to compare them with the ones on this page, which were made up by poets. Ask them to think up similes which no one else has used.

Developing Literacy
Poetry Compendium:
Ages 7–11
© A & C BLACK

A simile poem

- **Read the poem.**
- **How would you describe yourself?**
- **On the notepad, list some adjectives you could use.**
- **Make up similes for them.**

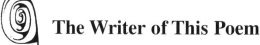

The Writer of This Poem

The writer of this poem
Is taller than a tree
As keen as the North wind
As handsome as can be

As bold as a boxing-glove
As sharp as a nib
As strong as scaffolding
As tricky as a fib

As smooth as a lolly-ice
As quick as a lick
As clean as a chemist-shop
As clever as a ✓

The writer of this poem
Never ceases to amaze
He's one in a million billion
(or so the poem says!)

Roger McGough

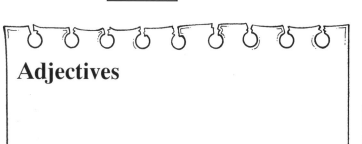

Adjectives

Similes

- **Make up your own version of the poem.**

The writer of this poem

Is _____

As _____

As _____

Write other verses
on the back of
this page. Your poem
need not rhyme.

- **Read your poem with a partner.**
- **Find ways to improve it.**

Teachers' note The children could brainstorm adjectives to use and, with a partner, make up similes based on them. Model some examples: as gentle as a teddy bear, as funny as a clown, as sporty as a footballer, as graceful as a swallow, as gentle as a cat's paw. Encourage the children to type out their own versions of the poem for display.

**Developing Literacy
Poetry Compendium:
Ages 7–11
© A & C BLACK**

A poem from the past

John Bunyan wrote this poem in the seventeenth century.

- **Underline the words which show that it was written more than 300 years ago.**

Upon the Snail

She goes but softly, but she goeth sure;
　　She stumbles not as stronger creatures do:
Her journey's shorter, so she may endure
　　Better than they which do much further go.

She makes no noise, but stilly seizeth on
　　The flower or herb appointed for her food,
The which she quietly doth feed upon,
　　While others range and gare*, but find no good.

And though she doth but very softly go,
　　However 'tis not fast, nor slow, but sure;
And certainly they that do travel so,
　　The prize they aim at, they do procure.

gare – stare all around

- **Write the words from the poem which mean:**

goes _____ does not stumble _____

calmly _____ seizes _____

chosen _____ feeds _____

does _____ it is _____

- **Write down what these words mean.**

Use a dictionary.

procure _____ endure _____

Now try this!

- **List all the verbs in the poem.**
- **Describe what is unusual about many of them.**

Look for two ways in which the verbs are unusual.

Teachers' note Read the poem while the children listen. Read it again, and ask them to put up their hands when you come to a word we no longer use. Give them the opportunity to deduce the meanings of these words before explaining them.

**Developing Literacy
Poetry Compendium:
Ages 7–11
© A & C BLACK**

Rhyme choice

- **Fill in the gaps in the poem.**
  Choose from the words
  on the notepad.

Think about rhymes which make sense and help to create the best effects.

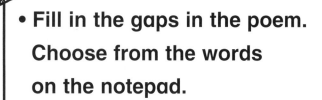

Windy Nights

Whenever the moon and stars are set,

   Whenever the wind is high,

All night long in the dark and _____,

   A man goes riding _____,

Late in the night when the fires are out,

Why does he gallop and gallop _____?

Whenever the trees are crying aloud,

And the ships are tossed at _____,

By, on the highway, low and _____,

By at the gallop goes _____,

By at the gallop he goes, and then

By he comes back at the gallop _____,

Robert Louis Stevenson

Word-bank

about
and shout
by
get
the sky
throughout
wet
why

again
amen
at ten
free
he
loud
proud
sea
she
to men
yet

 Now try this!

- **Explain your choices**
  of rhyming words.
- **Read the poem aloud.**
- **Does it sound right?**

You might want to change some of the words you chose.

Teachers' note Ask the children to read the poem aloud with their group or with a partner and to discuss which is the best word to fill each gap. Ask the children to describe the rhyme pattern of the poem: alternate lines except for the last two lines of each verse, which are a rhyming couplet.

Developing Literacy
Poetry Compendium:
Ages 7–11
© A & C BLACK

Fantastic football

- **Complete the** alliterative **football headlines.**

Include the name of the team, an adjective and a noun or verb.

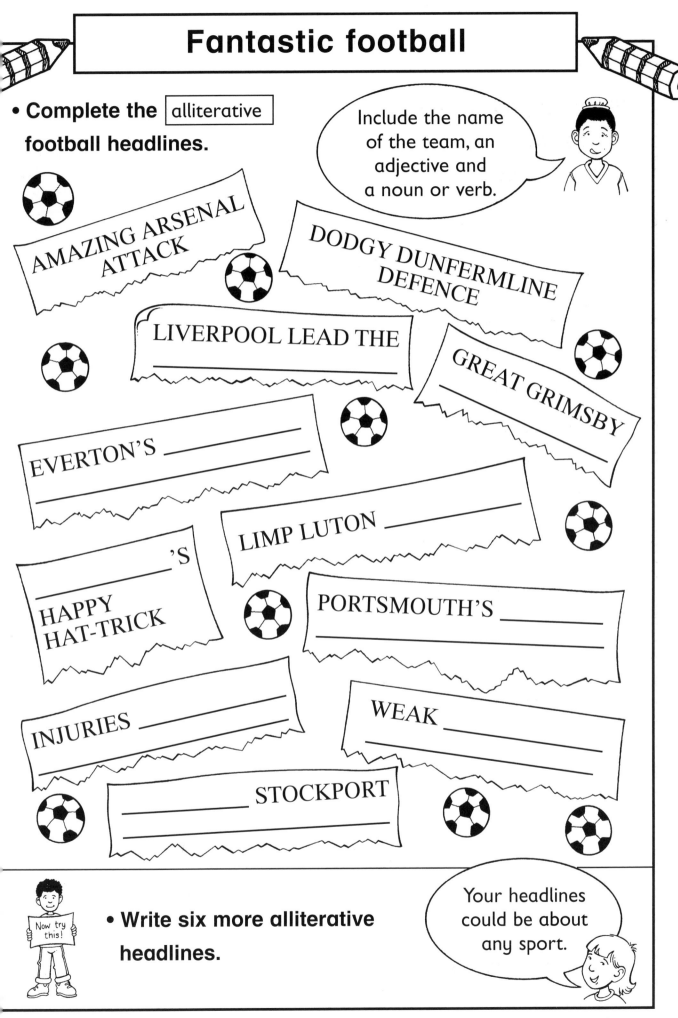

AMAZING ARSENAL ATTACK

DODGY DUNFERMLINE DEFENCE

LIVERPOOL LEAD THE _____

GREAT GRIMSBY _____

EVERTON'S _____

_____'S

LIMP LUTON _____

HAPPY HAT-TRICK

PORTSMOUTH'S _____

INJURIES _____

WEAK _____

_____ STOCKPORT

- **Write six more alliterative headlines.**

Now try this!

Your headlines could be about any sport.

Developing Literacy
Poetry Compendium:
Ages 7–11
© A & C BLACK

Teachers' note Read the completed headlines with the children and complete some different ones with them on the board: for example, CHARLTON CHASE THE CHAMPIONSHIP, READING ROUT ROCHDALE. Provide lists of football clubs (available on the Football Association website). Introduce the activity by brainstorming football match ideas or even showing a short video clip of a match.

A skylark sang

- **Read the poem aloud.**
  Listen for | alliteration |.
- **Write the groups of words with alliteration in each verse.**

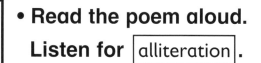

A Green Cornfield

The earth was green, the sky was blue:
I saw and heard one sunny morn
A skylark hang between the two,
A singing speck above the corn;

A stage below, in gay accord,
White butterflies danced on the wing,
And still the singing skylark soared,
And silent sank and soared to sing.

The cornfield stretched a tender green
To right and left beside my walks;
I knew he had a nest unseen
Somewhere among the million stalks.

And as I paused to hear his song
While swift the sunny moments slid,
Perhaps his mate sat listening long,
And listened longer than I did.

Christina Rossetti

Verse 1

S

Verse 2

S

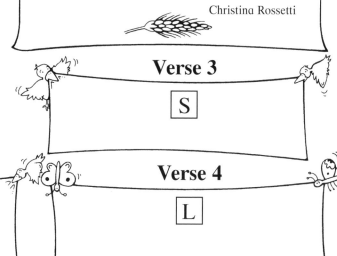

Verse 3

S

Verse 4

S

Verse 4

L

Now try this!

- **Describe the effects the poet creates by using alliteration.**

Teachers' note Read the poem aloud, emphasising the soaring, flying effects of the alliterative 's' sounds and the long, lingering 'l' sounds. Ask the children what impression the poem gives them of the skylark's movement, and of the poet.

**Developing Literacy
Poetry Compendium:
Ages 7–11
© A & C BLACK**

Morning

- **Read the poem.**
- **Underline the words which describe the sounds.**
- **List the sounds <u>you</u> hear in the morning.**
- **Think about what makes them.**

Morning comes
   with a milk-float jiggling

Morning comes
   with a milkman whistling

Morning comes
   with empties clinking

Morning comes
   with alarm-clock ringing

Morning comes
   with letters dropping

Morning comes
   with toaster popping

Morning comes
   with kettle singing

Morning comes
   with me just listening.

Morning comes to drag me out of
bed
   – Boss-Woman morning.

Grace Nichols

Sound	Made by
chirping	sparrow

Now try this!

- **Choose four sounds from your list.**
- **Use them in four new lines for the poem.**
- **Think about how the final line of the poem is different from the others.**
- **Write a different final line for the poem.**

Teachers' note The children should recognise which lines and parts of lines are repeated and which change. Ask them to imagine the scene described; brainstorm what else might be heard in the morning.

Developing Literacy
Poetry Compendium:
Ages 7–11
© A & C BLACK

Night

- **What do you hear at night as you lie in bed?**
- **Make notes.**

...an owl hooting

...car doors slamming

- **Write a poem entitled 'Night'.**

Night comes_____

Night comes_____

Night comes_____

Night comes_____

Night comes_____

Night comes_____

Now try this!

- **Read your poem aloud.**
- **In red, mark any changes you want to make.**

Work with a partner.

Teachers' note Encourage the children to prepare for this activity at home, by jotting down the things they hear last thing at night (at that stage their jottings should be in note form, with no attempt to write a poem, but they should say what makes the sound, and use a verb which describes it). They could type out their poems for display.

Developing Literacy Poetry Compendium: Ages 7–11 © A & C BLACK

School poem

Use a thesaurus.

- **Read the first four lines of the poem.**
- **What do you notice about the teachers' names and the verbs?** _____

_____

- **Capture the escaped verbs and write them in the gaps.**

At the End of School Assembly

Miss Sparrow's lot flew out,
Mrs Steed's lot galloped out,
Mr Bull's lot got herded out,
Mrs Bumble's lot buzzed off.

Miss Rose's class... rose,
Mr Beetle's class... beetled off,

Miss Storm's class _____ ,

Mrs Frisby's class _____ ,

Mr Train's lot _____ ,

Miss Ferry's lot _____ ,

Mr Roller's lot _____ ,

Mrs Street's lot got stuck halfway across.

Mr Idle's class _____ ,

Mrs Barrow's class _____ ,

Miss Stretcher's class _____ ,

And Mr Brook's class

Simply _____ .

Simon Pitt

sailed out

were carried out

got their skates on

couldn't be bothered

were wheeled out

trickled away

made tracks

whirled across the hall

thundered out

- **Make up lines for these teachers.**

Now try this!

| Ms Worm | Mr Ballet | Mrs Gunn | Miss Pony |

Teachers' note The children should notice the links between the teachers' names and the verbs: ask them to explain how the poet chose the verbs. The children might need to look up some of the words. Some children might be able to make up names for other teachers as well as their classes' actions.

Developing Literacy
Poetry Compendium:
Ages 7–11
© A & C BLACK

Write a mystery poem

• **Use this page to plan a mystery poem.**

Subject of the mystery

_____

Ideas

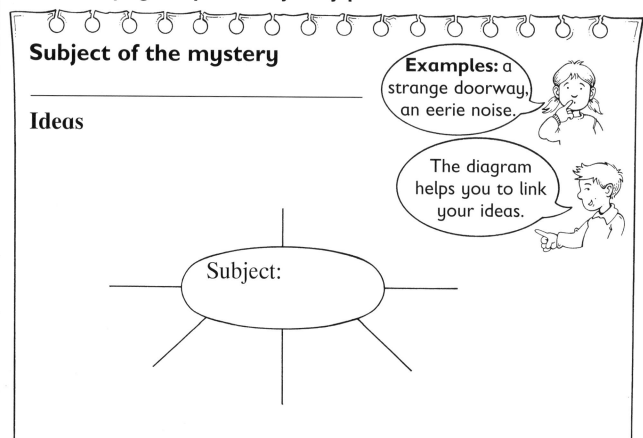

Examples: a strange doorway, an eerie noise.

The diagram helps you to link your ideas.

Subject:

Useful words

Nouns	Verbs	Adjectives

Use a dictionary.

Use a thesaurus.

Underline any ideas for rhyme or alliteration.

Teachers' note Before beginning this activity the children need to have read mystery poems: for example, 'The Visitor' by Ian Serraillier, 'The Listeners' by Walter de la Mare, 'The Oak Chest' by Fred Sedgwick and 'The Two Old Women of Mumbling Hill' by James Reeves. Revise ideas for creating effects by the use of words and rhythm.

Developing Literacy
Poetry Compendium:
Ages 7–11
© A & C BLACK

Haiku

A 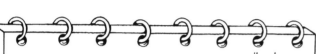haiku has seventeen

syllables arranged in three lines.

It should be about something in nature.

- **Read these notes for a haiku.**
- **On the chart, list the changes.**
- **Explain the changes.**

Underground, burrowing ~~digging~~

with h~~is~~ ~~great~~ paws. *tirelessly busy*

The mole ~~is going~~ home. *heads for*

Under ground, digging

with tirelessly busy paws,

the mole heads for home.

Change	Reason
_____	_____
_____	_____
_____	_____
_____	_____
_____	_____
_____	_____

- **Read other haiku.**
- **Count the syllables in each line.**

Now try this!

- **Write your own haiku.**

It should be about something in nature.

Teachers' note Discuss the example haiku with the children and ask them to identify and explain the first change made by the writer. Encourage them to read aloud the first version ('Underground burrowing') and then the changed version ('Under ground, digging) and to describe the difference. Discuss the arrangement of the seventeen syllables, in three lines of five, seven and five.

Developing Literacy
Poetry Compendium:
Ages 7–11
© A & C BLACK

Writing a tanka

A ⟦tanka⟧ is a poem about an event in nature.

- **Read the tanka.**
- **List some subjects for tanka.**

1 *a ray of sunlight shining through clouds*

2

3

4

5

Tanka 1

A pool of sunlight
Bathes the stormy evening bay.
A lonely heron
Stands still, a cunning statue,
Waiting for unwary fish.

John Kitching

A tanka has five lines of syllables in this order:

⟦ five ⟧ ⟦ seven ⟧ ⟦ five ⟧ ⟦ seven ⟧ ⟦ seven ⟧

- **Make notes for your own tanka.**

Subject: _____

line 1 _____

line 2 _____

line 3 _____

line 4 _____

line 5 _____

Now try this!

- **From your notes, write a tanka.**
- **Read it aloud to a partner.**
- **Count the syllables and think about the words.**
- **Make changes if you need to.**

Teachers' note An effective introduction would be to show a short video of natural events such as sunrise, sunset, a duck taking off or landing on water, a bird singing, seeds falling from a flower, birds in a bird bath, a cat stretching or sunlight on a cornfield or on a patch of greenery in a city.

**Developing Literacy
Poetry Compendium:
Ages 7–11
© A & C BLACK**

Cinquain consequences

A cinquain has twenty-two syllables.

line 1 – two syllables
line 2 – four syllables
line 3 – six syllables
line 4 – eight syllables
line 5 – two syllables

'Cinq' is the French word for 'five'. A cinquain has five lines.

1. Cut out the card below.

2. Player 1 writes line 1 (two syllables): the name of a person or thing.

3. Player 2 writes line 2 (four syllables): what the person or thing did or said.

4. Player 3 writes line 3 (six syllables): where it happened.

5. Player 4 writes lines 4 and 5 (eight and two syllables): why he, she or it did it or what happened as a result.

6. Open out your **Cinquain consequences** and read the cinquain aloud.

7. Check that each line has the correct number of syllables.

Each player folds the paper under so that the next one cannot see what is written on it.

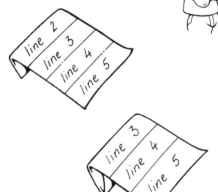

Cinquain consequences

line 1	
line 2	
line 3	
line 4	
line 5	

Teachers' note Read some cinquains with the children (see **Notes on the activities**, pages 38–39) and ask them to describe their structure: the number of lines and the number of syllables in each line. What do they notice about the last line (its syllables and the kind of thing it says)? The children could also write their own cinquains.

Developing Literacy
Poetry Compendium:
Ages 7–11
© A & C BLACK

List poems

This is one kind of | list poem |.
It is based on a train journey.

- On the chart, write what you notice
  about its | structure | and | rhythm |.

This is the
Nine-fifteen
Trans-Pennine train:
Newcastle,
Sunderland,
Darlington and York,
Durham and
Huddersfield,
Manchester and Leeds,
Warrington
and Runcorn,
Liverpool at last.

Number of verses or stanzas _____

Number of lines _____

Syllable pattern

Line 1: 3   Line 2:   Line :   Line :   Line :   Line :

Line 7:   Line :   :   :   :   :

- **Describe how the syllable
  pattern is repeated.**

_____

_____

Read the poem aloud.
Clap the syllables.

- **Try arranging the place names in different ways.**
- **What happens to the rhythm?**
- **Change the beginning and ending.**
- **Have you improved the poem, or do you
  like the original better?**

Teachers' note Read the example and other list poems with the children. Point out that there
is usually an introduction followed by the items in the list, which should be linked in some way:
for example, colours or different types of the same thing. Discuss the structure of the poems:
the numbers of verses or stanzas and lines and any repeated pattern of syllables line by line.

**Developing Literacy
Poetry Compendium:
Ages 7–11
© A & C BLACK**

A 'thin' poem

- **Read the poem aloud.**
- **What does its** rhythm **remind you of?**

_____

- **What do the first two lines of the poem tell you?**

_____

_____

- **Count the syllables in lines 3 to 15.**
- **What do you notice?**

_____

_____

- **Underline the words which remind you of a clock.**

Dandelion Time

Dandelion
Clock tower.
No bell
To tell
The hour.

No tick,
No chime,
No face
To trace
The time.

No glass,
No sands.
Time blown,
Not shown
By hands.

Sue Cowling

- **Make notes to help you to write a 'thin' poem about time.**

Your title could be *Sundial, Egg timer, Stop-watch, Candle* or *Wristwatch.*

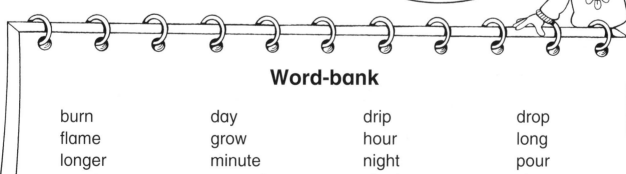

Word-bank

burn	day	drip	drop
flame	grow	hour	long
longer	minute	night	pour
quartz	second	shadow	short
shorter	shrink	sound	spring

Teachers' note The children could rearrange the poem as prose and read it aloud. What difference does this make to the way in which they read it? How does it affect the rhythm of the poem? Encourage the children to type out their 'thin' poems for display.

Developing Literacy Poetry Compendium: Ages 7–11 © A & C BLACK

Alphabetical haunted castle

• **Complete this alphabetical poem about a haunted castle.**

 Make it scary!

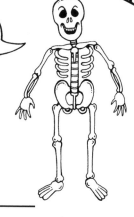

A is for 'aagh', alarmed and afraid,

B is for 'boo', banshees and beasts,

C is for creaking _____

D _____

E is for 'eek' and eerie _____

F _____

G is for genie _____

H _____

I _____

J is for jitters _____

K _____

L _____

M is for magic and mystery at midnight,

N _____

O is for omens _____

P is for phantom _____

Q _____

R _____

S is for spectre _____

T _____

 Now try this!

• **Continue the alphabet.**

Word-bank

UFO   ugly   unearthly   vampire

werewolf   weird   zombie

Teachers' note During the introductory session brainstorm words connected with hauntings and ghosts. The children could arrange them in an alphabetical word-bank. After sharing their alphabetical poems during the plenary session, they could compile a class poem based on the best ideas from all of them.

Developing Literacy Poetry Compendium: Ages 7–11
© A & C BLACK

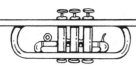

A conversation poem

- • **Work in a group.**
- • **Read the poem.**
- • **Complete the notes for another poem with the title:**

Who broke the window?

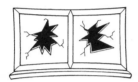

Notes

Questions

Who broke the window?

_____

_____

_____

Answers

I, said Paul, with my little ball

_____

_____

_____

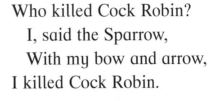

Who killed Cock Robin?
  I, said the Sparrow,
   With my bow and arrow,
I killed Cock Robin.

Who saw him die?
  I, said the Fly,
   With my little eye,
I saw him die.

Who caught his blood?
  I, said the Fish,
   With my little dish,
I caught his blood.

From *An Elegy on the
Death and Burial of Cock Robin*
Anonymous

- • **Use your notes to help you to write a poem: *Who broke the window?***

Teachers' note If possible, read with the children the whole of *An Elegy on the Death and Burial of Cock Robin* (in *The Oxford Nursery Rhyme Book* by Iona and Peter Opie). What do they notice about the first and last lines of each verse? The whole class or group could read the opening question of each verse, and different children could read the words of the different characters.

Developing Literacy
Poetry Compendium:
Ages 7–11
© A & C BLACK

A monologue

This poem is a
monologue .

'Mono' means single.

My Heart's in the Highlands

My heart's in the Highlands, my heart is not here;
My heart's in the Highlands a-chasing the deer;
Chasing the wild deer and following the roe;
My heart's in the Highlands, wherever I go.
Farewell to the Highlands, farewell to the North,
The birthplace of valour, the country of worth;
Wherever I wander, wherever I rove,
The hills of the Highlands for ever I love.

Farewell to the mountains, high-covered with snow;
Farewell to the straths* and green valleys below;
Farewell to the forests and wild-hanging woods;
Farewell to the torrents and loud-pouring floods.
My heart's in the Highlands, my heart is not here;
My heart's in the Highlands a-chasing the deer;
Chasing the wild deer and following the roe;
My heart's in the Highlands, wherever I go.

Robert Burns

*strath – a Scottish word for a broad river valley surrounded by high ground

- **In which person is the poem written?** ✓

  First person ☐

  Second person ☐

  Third person ☐

- **Underline the words which tell you this.**

- **Write what the poet is saying about his feelings.** _____

  _____

  _____

- **Write the words which tell you this.**

  _____

  _____

Now try this!

- **List, in your own words, everything the poet loves about the Highlands.**

Teachers' note Introduce the activity by reading the poem with the children and comparing it with other poems which are not monologues (for example, on pages 42, 44 and 50). Ask the children how a monologue differs from other poems and ask them to support their answers by quoting words from the poems.

Developing Literacy
Poetry Compendium:
Ages 7–11
© A & C BLACK

Prayers: 1

1

Let freedom ring...!
Allow freedom to ring...!
from every mountainside...
from every peak
from every village and
hamlet.

From *I have a dream...*
by Martin Luther King

2

We return thanks to our mother, the earth,
which sustains us.
We return thanks to the rivers and streams,
which supply us with water.
We return thanks to all herbs, which furnish
medicines for the cure of our diseases.

From *An Iroquois Prayer* (Anonymous)

3

Blessed, praised and glorified
be the name of the Holy One,
blessed be He.
He who makes peace in His high places,
may He make peace for us
and for all Israel, and say Amen.

Kaddish, *a Jewish prayer*

4

God be in my head
And in my understanding.
God be in my eyes
And in my looking.
God be in my mouth
And in my speaking.

From *God be in my Head*
(Anonymous)

5

...forgive us our trespasses,
as we forgive those
who trespass against us...

From *The Lord's Prayer*
(The Alternative Service Book)

6

Oh, give us pleasure in the orchard white;
Like nothing else by day, like ghosts by night;
And make us happy in the happy bees,
The swarm dilating round the perfect trees.

From *A Prayer in Spring* by Robert Frost

7

Bring me now where the warm wind
glows, where the grasses
sigh, where the sweet
tongued blossom flowers

From *Slow Guitar*
by Edward Kamau Brathwaite

8

Dear Lord and Father of Mankind,
Forgive our foolish ways!
Re-clothe us in our rightful mind,
In purer lives thy service find,
In deeper reverence praise.

From *Dear Lord and Father of Mankind*
by John Whittier

9

Everything in the Universe is peaceful;
peace is everywhere.
May that peace come to me.

From a *Hindu Hymn of Peace*
(*The Shanti Path*) (Anonymous)

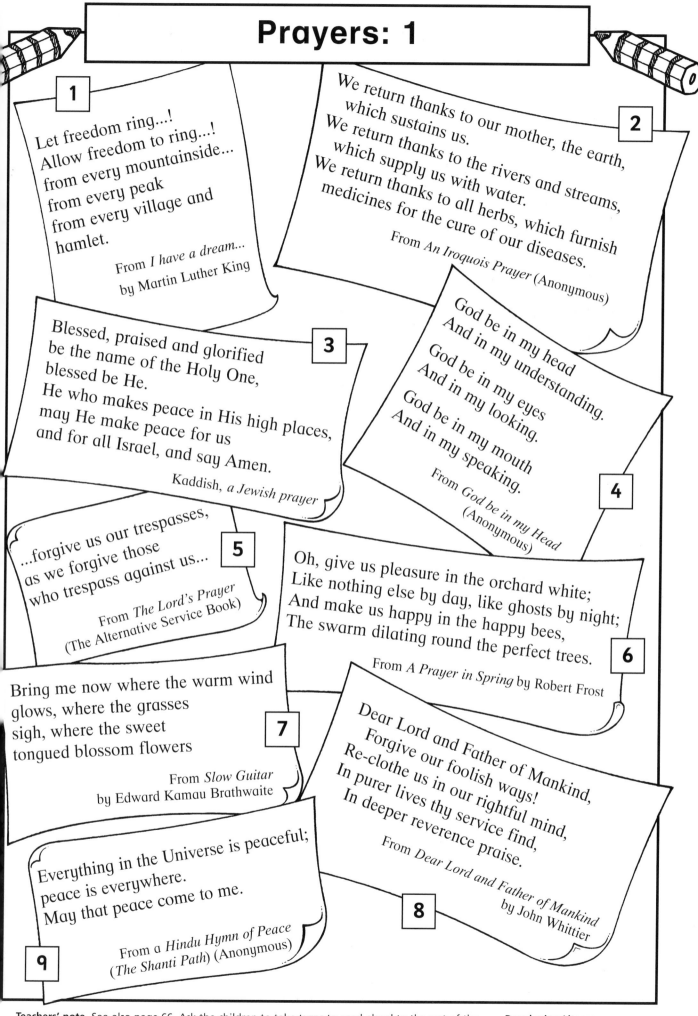

Teachers' note See also page 66. Ask the children to take turns to read aloud to the rest of the class one of the extracts from prayers. Ask them what makes prayers different from other poems. Are they always addressed to God? If not, to whom might a prayer be addressed? The children could read other prayers and add them to the chart on page 66.

**Developing Literacy
Poetry Compendium:
Ages 7–11
© A & C BLACK**

Prayers: 2

- **Read each [prayer] and discuss with your group.**

Think about: its purpose (why people say or sing it)

to whom or what it is said or sung.

Choose the most important words.

- **Write notes on the chart.**

Prayer	Purpose	Words which show this	To whom or what it is said or sung	Words which show this
1	to ask for something	let, allow	We cannot tell	
2				
3				
4				
5				
6				
7				
8				
9				

- **Underline the verbs in the prayers.**
- **What do you notice about them?**

Now try this!

Teachers' note This should be used with page 65. To allow more space, enlarge the page to A3. The children should notice the various purposes of prayers. Ask them for what people might give thanks in their prayers, what or whom they might praise, for what they might ask or want to be forgiven.

**Developing Literacy
Poetry Compendium:
Ages 7–11**
© A & C BLACK

Epitaphs

- **Read the** epitaphs.
- **What do they tell you?**
- **Copy and complete the chart.**

An epitaph talks about someone or something which has died.

1
Stranger, approach this spot with gravity: John Brown is filling his last cavity.

2
Here lies the body of Ezra Pound, Lost at sea and never found.

3
Here lies, whom hound did n'er pursue. Nor swifter greyhound follow...
William Cowper

4
Beneath this stone A lump of clay Lies Arabella Young Who on the 21st of May 1771 Began to hold her tongue.

5
Here lies a great and mighty king whose promise none relies on; He never said a foolish thing Nor ever did a wise one.

6
Here a pretty baby lies Sung asleep with lullabies; Pray be silent, and not stir Th'easy earth that covers her.
Robert Herrick

Epitaph	Sad or Funny	What it tells the reader about the dead person or animal
1		
2		

Now try this!

- **Begin an anthology of epitaphs.**
- **Write about when each was written and for whom or what they were written.**

Teachers' note It hardly needs saying that this topic requires sensitive handling or, if a child has experienced a death in the family, perhaps should not be done at all. Read the epitaphs with the children: some of the words need to be explained, as does the purpose of an epitaph – to say something about someone or something which has died (see **Notes on the activities**, page 39).

Developing Literacy
Poetry Compendium:
Ages 7–11
© A & C BLACK

Notes on the activities

The notes below expand upon those provided at the bottom of the activity pages. They give ideas and suggestions for making the most of the activity sheet, including suggestions for the whole-class introduction, the plenary session or for follow-up work using an adapted version of the sheet. To help teachers to select appropriate learning experiences for their pupils, the activities are grouped into units in line with the Primary Framework for Literacy, but the pages need not be presented in the order in which they appear, unless stated otherwise.

Unit 1: Poetic style

The activities in this section increase the range of poetry the children know so that they can discuss likes and dislikes. They also develop the children's understanding of the devices and forms which give particular poets their unique style and the ways in which poets convey meaning by their choice of words. They also help the children to develop their own style by learning to work with metaphor, rhyme, alliteration and other effects, and in selecting words to convey feelings or impressions.

Shakespeare's sounds (page 72). 'Ariel's Song' develops the children's appreciation of the ways in which poets use words to create effects. Explain that *The Tempest* was set on an island after a shipwreck. The song presents death as a beautiful and mysterious transformation. Discuss the way in which Shakespeare's words convey this impression: 'coral', 'pearls' and 'a sea-change / Into something rich and strange'.

All the world's a stage (page 73). This extract from Jaques' 'Seven Ages of Man' speech from Shakespeare's *As You Like It* develops the children's ability to distinguish between comparison and metaphor. It introduces them to the idea of the sustained metaphor: in this case connected with the theatre. Revise the use of similes (see pages 47–48) for comparisons using 'like' or 'as' and discuss the difference between similes and metaphors: a

metaphor says that the person or thing being compared is not *like* something else but actually *is* something else. During the plenary session invite the children to share their answers. They should have found the following 'theatre metaphor' words: stage (the world), players (men and women), exits, entrances, plays, parts and acts.

Sonnet (page 74). Here the children learn to recognise the structure of a sonnet: it has fourteen lines and its usual rhyme scheme is *abbaabba*, followed by two or three other rhymes in the remaining six lines. Another common rhyme scheme is *ababcdcdefefgg*. Explain to the children what these letters represent in terms of rhyme. Provide other poems (including sonnets by Shakespeare) for the children to check to see if they *are* sonnets. Ask them to notice any common themes in the sonnets they read. They can then use the sonnet as a model for their own.

Two seaside poems: 1 and **2** (pages 75–76). This activity presents two twentieth-century poems which use a similar story and setting to convey a similar message: that people's actions reveal their true souls. The children are encouraged to notice differences between the two poets' styles: in the first poem E. E. Cummings uses very little punctuation and only one capital letter and the rhyme pattern of each verse changes (they might notice that although the two lines of verses 1, 3, 5 and 6 rhyme (or half rhyme), the lines of verses 2 and 4 do not, but they half rhyme with, or repeat, one another: 'sang'/'thing', 'and'/'and'). The second poem, by James Reeves, has a simpler and more traditional rhyme scheme: the second and fourth lines of each verse. This could be linked with work on character studies: the children could write a character profile of one of the children in either poem.

Seaside poem writer (page 77). The children are given a framework to write a poem about characters about whom they have read, following the structure of one of the poems on page 75. They could either write a new poem using the structure of one of those poems or copy some of the poem, changing some of the words or lines. The activity sheet asks the children to list words they could use in their poems: they should try to find words which will help to reveal the character of each person in the poem.

E. Cummings: **1** and **2** (pages 78–79). This helps to increase the range of poems the children know. It provides another poem by E. E. Cummings (see also page 75). It is a good example of the stylistic freedom provided by poetry: there are no constraints of rhyme or rhythm (these devices can be used to create whatever effects are wanted). The children should notice that there are no capital letters at the beginnings of lines (the only capital letters used are for the word 'Just' in line 1 and within the word 'balloonMan') and there is no punctuation. The activities draw attention to the way in which E. E. Cummings uses spacing, structure and avoidance of punctuation to create the pace and rhythm of the poem. Point out the way in which the spacing of 'whistles   far   and   wee' makes the sound of the balloon man's whistle seem to float away into the air, while the closely-printed 'eddieandbill' is fast like their running and 'bettyandisbel' is fast like their dancing. Before the children do the activity on page 79, talk about hyphenated words, compound words and internal rhyme (rhyme within the same line of poetry). The activity encourages them to make up their own words to create internal rhyme effects by joining other words in the way in which E. E. Cummings does (for example, 'mud-luscious' and 'puddle-wonderful').

A poem without rhyme (page 80). 'The Song of Life' poem comes from the Côte d'Ivoire. The structure and patterns of the poem help to convey the idea that life is a cycle (point out that it starts and ends with the same word).

Free verse (page 81). This activity develops the children's appreciation of the differences between free verse and other types of poetry and between free verse and prose. They should notice the way in which the use of new lines in this poem affects the rhythm of their reading, and how it creates pauses which break up the poem and separate the ideas presented in it. They should also notice the repetitive pattern: 'Doondari created…' , '… defeated…'. The Fulani or Fulah are a people who live mainly in desert areas of Nigeria. Doondari and Gueno are their gods.

Two poets: research (page 82). The children can use this sheet to compare the work of any two poets they have studied; it helps them to organise their ideas.

Unit 2: Classic/narrative poems

This section introduces the form of the longer narrative poem. The children investigate poetic devices such as pace, rhythm and rhyme used to create dramatic effects. Encourage them to perform these poems aloud, to keep a record of their responses and to discuss these regularly in their groups or with the whole class.

Tell the story (page 83). In this story poem, the children should notice the way in which the lengths of the lines change with the rhyme pattern and thus change the rhythm of the poem. It can be split into three sections on the basis of rhyme and rhythm, ending with lines 4, 20 and 25. Point out the way in which the lines are paired for rhyme in the middle section: 'hard' refers to 'ground' but it rhymes with 'yard' (but there is no rhyme with 'wooden'; 'England', in the next line, does not rhyme with anything). The effect of this rhyme pattern is to link one idea to the next. In the extension activity, the main points of the story which the children should mention are: that the boy seemed to think that he would have a better time in Scotland than in England but when he got there he found that things were just the same, and then he wondered whether running away had been worthwhile. Point out the positioning of important words at the ends of lines to emphasise them. The children could also write or key in the text and arrange it in long lines or as prose, read it aloud and notice the difference made by the layout.

Travellers' tales: 1 and **2** (pages 84–85). These are contrasting narrative poems about journeys on horseback. Compare the stories behind the two poems: the first has an urgency which is reflected in the fast pace and the galloping rhythm, while the second has a mysterious atmosphere whose silence is broken only by the traveller's knocking on the door. *How They Brought the Good News from Ghent to Aix* can be found in several anthologies, including *Classic Poems to Read Aloud* (Kingfisher).

A fox and a stag: 1 and **2** (pages 86–87). These are two poems about animals being hunted. The first creates the impression that the reader is riding with the hunters: the stag is always ahead and there is little detail about him (just an air of grace and grandeur), and the poem is written in the first person plural (we – the hunters). The feelings conveyed by the poet at the end of the poem seem to be mixed: there is a tinge of regret that the stag got away from them, mixed with sorrow that he drowned, and compassion: '… slept at last in a jewelled bed'. In contrast, the second poem creates the impression that the reader is running with the fox and can almost feel his weariness and breathlessness: the hunters are always behind him and there is close-up detail about the fox, while the hunters are less distinct, and the poem is written in the third person singular (he – the fox). This detail, together with the impact of the rhythm – the breathless pace of the poem – conveys the feeling that the poet is willing the fox to keep running, and the reader is caught up in this feeling. This activity could be linked with non-fiction work on persuasive writing.

Speed, rhythm and rhyme: 1 and **2** (pages 88–89). This activity develops the children's ability to appreciate the effect of the rhythm and pace of a long narrative poem. They should notice the repetition of certain lines. This repetition evokes the surging charge of the men in battle; it is as if the charge goes on and on throughout the poem. The change in rhythm in verses 1 to 5 comes at lines 7, 16, 24, 37 and 48 respectively. It separates the description of the action from the poet's reflections on the event. It begins with a regular rhythm of 'galloping horses' and then begins to stumble, as the horses did in battle.

Narrative poetry log (page 90). This provides a framework to help the children to record their personal responses to narrative poems they read. The log (and additional copies, if needed) could be kept in the children's poetry files or exercise books and shared during discussions from time to time.

Unit 3: Choral and performance

This section encourages the children to consider the different ways in which poems can be read aloud (including the use of different numbers of voices for different parts of the poem), helps them to write their own performance poems and develops their skills in improving their poetry.

Read it aloud (page 91). This poem from Djibouti in Africa should be read by one voice (the clue is that it is written in the first person). It should sound strong (the children should notice the strong-sounding imagery such as: 'mountains as my footstool', 'I cup lakes in my palms' and 'I fling oceans around me like a shawl'). It should be read slowly so as to sound powerful, dignified and even mysterious, and the rhythm should be flowing, like a strong river (suggested by the changing lengths of the lines, which gradually lengthen and then shorten). When the reading has been completed, ask the children who they think Mawu is.

Rap and **Rap writer** (pages 92–93). These activities develop the children's appreciation of the rhythm of a rap. They should try to write lines with the same numbers of syllables as the original. Put all their

verses together to produce a class rap. The extension activity on page 93 helps the children to write a verse to introduce the rap; they could also write a verse to end it. They could practise their rap and then perform it for the rest of the school. During the performance each child could step forward to read his or her verse and the whole class could read the introductory and final verses.

A poem to perform: 1 and **2** (pages 94–95). These pages provide a structure on which the children can plan a new verse for 'Baa, Baa, Black Sheep' and then make notes for younger children about how to perform it. If necessary, provide a copy of the original nursery rhyme, from which the children can see the rhyming pattern.

Conversation poem: 1 (page 96). In the conversation poem 'The Visitor', the children use their voices to represent different speakers and the narrator and to show the speakers' feelings. It will be helpful to discuss the structure of the poem and how the poet sets the scene: the first and last verses have three lines, while the others have two. Discuss the way in which the feelings of the woman in the poem change (and can be shown in her tone of voice), from delight with the lovely ring, to puzzlement when she first hears the voice of the skeleton, and finally to terror as the skeleton tears the bedclothes from her grasp. Note also the man's feelings as he reassures his wife – "It'll soon go away" – until the skeleton tears off the bedclothes, and then the climax of his fear, in the words "THROW IT AWAY!" Point out the sudden change of tone: the skeleton clattered downhill and 'all was still'.

Conversation poem: 2 (page 97). The children write a story poem told through a conversation; their poems can be modelled on the structure of 'The Visitor' (page 96) but could tell *any* kind of story. If they follow the rhyme structure of 'The Visitor', discourage them from making rhyme the main issue: the important thing is to tell the story as a conversation with a good rhythm. They could read their poem aloud and evaluate it with a partner, and then rearrange it and substitute rhyming words. Provide thesauruses and rhyming dictionaries. The children could write (or type) the final version of their poem and mark it to help them to read it aloud (for example, by underlining in different colours to show change of speaker and double underlining stressed words or syllables).

Learning objectives

The following chart shows how the Ages 9–10 activity sheets (pages 72–97) match the learning objectives addressed by the Year 5 units in the Poetry block of the Primary Framework for Literacy. (Where a page number is shown in bold type, this indicates the learning objective is the main focus of the activity.)

Objectives	Unit 1: Poetic style	Unit 2: Classic/ narrative poems	Unit 3: Choral and performance
Group discussion and interaction			
Plan and manage a group task over time using different levels of planning		83	91, 93, 96
Understand different ways to take the lead and support others in groups		83	93, 96
Drama			
Use and recognise the impact of theatrical effects in drama	72, 73	83	91, **92**, 94–96
Understanding and interpreting texts			
Make notes on and use evidence from across a text to explain events or ideas	72–74, **75**, **76**, 78, 79, **80**, **81**	**83**, **84**, 85, 86, 81, 88	96
Infer writers' perspectives from what is written and from what is implied	76, 78, 79, **82**	**87**, **88**	
Explore how writers use language for comic and dramatic effects	**72**, **73**, **74**, 75, **78**, **79**	84, **85**, 86, **89**, **90**	**91**, 92, 96, 97
Engaging with and responding to texts			
Reflect on reading habits and preferences and plan personal reading goals	82	85, **86**, 90	
Compare the usefulness of techniques, such as visualisation, prediction, empathy in exploring the meaning of texts	76	81, 88	91
Compare how a common theme is presented in poetry, prose and other media	74, 75, 76, 82	84–88	
Creating and shaping texts			
Reflect independently and critically on own writing and edit and improve it	**77**		**93**, **94**, **95**, **97**
Adapt non-narrative forms and styles to write fiction or factual texts, including poems			93–95, **96**, 97

Shakespeare's sounds

- **Read the questions with a partner.**
- **Write your answers below.**

1. What does this line tell you has happened?

2. What do you notice about the sound of the words? What effect does this give? *Sauin attention — creates rhythm and mood.*

3. What usually happens to the bodies of the dead?

4. What special thing has happened to this one?

5. Which word in Line 2 and which word in Line 3 give the impression of beauty and riches?

6. Which words in Lines 5 and 6 create an air of mystery?

7. Describe these sounds. Are they loud, quiet, fast, slow, merry, sad, stately, mysterious …?

8. Do the bells clang, chime, peal, tinkle, clash, jingle …?

Ariel's Song

Full fathom five thy father lies;
   Of his bones are coral made;
Those are pearls that were his eyes:
   Nothing of him that doth fade
But doth suffer a sea-change
Into something rich and strange.
Sea-nymphs hourly ring his knell:
   Ding-dong!
Hark! now I hear them, –
Ding-dong, bell!

from *The Tempest*
by William Shakespeare

1. _____

2. _____

3. _____

4. _____

5. _____

6. _____

7. _____

8. _____

Now try this!

- **Write about the effect which Shakespeare created in 'Ariel's Song'.**
- **How did he create this effect?**

Teachers' note Read the poem aloud and explain some of the language: for example 'fathom'. Can the children work out what 'full fathom five' means? What do they think sea-nymphs are? Do they know what coral is?

Developing Literacy Poetry Compendium: Ages 7–11 © A & C BLACK

CM1

All the world's a stage

- **Read the poem.**
- **Underline the** comparisons **in** blue .
- **Underline the** metaphors **in** red .
- **Answer the questions.**

1. What are the metaphors for:

the world? _____stage_____

men and women? _____players_____

2. With what type of place are the metaphors connected?

_____theatre_____

3. Which other five words are connected with this place?

_____exists- entrance- plays_____
_____parts- acts._____

4. By using these metaphors, what is Shakespeare saying about human life?

_____that is like a play_____
_____

5. Can you think of any of the remaining five 'ages of man'?

_____
_____
_____

The Seven Ages of Man

All the world's a stage,
And all the men and women merely
    players:
They have their exits and their
    entrances;
And one man in his time plays
    many parts,
His acts being seven ages. At first
    the infant,
Mewling and puking in the nurse's
    arms.
And then the whining school-boy,
    with his satchel
And shining morning face, creeping
    like snail
Unwillingly to school.

from *As You Like It*
by William Shakespeare

- **List other words connected with the theatre.**
- **Use them in metaphors about events in your own life.**

Teachers' note Discuss comparisons and metaphor, pointing out that in a comparison or simile a person or thing is compared with something else (using the word 'like' or 'as'), whereas a metaphor says that the person or thing *is* something else.

Developing Literacy
Poetry Compendium:
Ages 7–11
© A & C BLACK

Sonnet

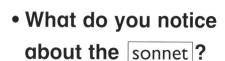

- **What do you notice about the** sonnet **?**
- **Make notes.**

Theme	
Addressed to	
Message	
Number of lines	
Rhyme pattern	

Sonnet

Remember me when I am gone away.
  Gone far away into the silent land:
  When you can no more hold me by the hand,
Nor I half turn to go yet turning stay.
Remember me when no more day by day
  You tell me of our future that you planned:
  Only remember me; you understand
It will be late to counsel then or pray.
Yet if you should forget me for a while
  And afterwards remember, do not grieve:
  For if the darkness and corruption leave
  A vestige of the thoughts that once I had,
Better by far that you should forget and smile
Than that you should remember and be sad.

Christina Rossetti

Label Line 1 and other lines which rhyme with it **a**. Label Line 2 and its rhyming lines **b** and so on.

- **Read other sonnets, and complete the chart.**

Title	Poet	Theme	Number of lines	Rhyme pattern

§Now try this!§

- **Write a set of instructions for writing a sonnet.**

Teachers' note Read this and other sonnets aloud but do not explain what distinguishes a sonnet from other types of poetry: the activity encourages the children to do that for themselves.

**Developing Literacy
Poetry Compendium:
Ages 7–11
© A & C BLACK**

Two seaside poems: 1

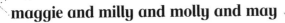

maggie and milly and molly and may

maggie and milly and molly and may
went down to the beach (to play one day)

and maggie discovered a shell that sang
so sweetly she couldn't remember her troubles,
   and

milly befriended a stranded star
whose rays five languid fingers were;

and molly was chased by a horrible thing
which raced sideways while blowing bubbles:
   and

may came home with a smooth round stone
as small as a world and as large as alone.

For whatever we lose (like a you or a me)
it's always ourselves we find in the sea

E. E. Cummings

- **Copy the chart.**
- **Record the similarities between the two poems.**

Similarity	Poem 1	Poem 2
Setting		
Story		
Poet's message		

- **Copy the chart.**
- **Record the differences between the two poems.**

Difference	Poem 1	Poem 2
Characters		
What they found		
Style: rhyme pattern punctuation		

The Black Pebble

There went three children down to the shore,
   Down to the shore and back;
There was skipping Susan and bright-eyed Sam
   And little scowling Jack.

Susan found a white cockle-shell,
   The prettiest ever seen,
And Sam picked up a piece of glass
   Rounded and smooth and green.

But Jack found only a plain black pebble
   That lay by the rolling sea
And that was all that ever he found;
   So back they went all three.

The cockle-shell they put on the table,
   The green glass on the shelf,
But the little black pebble that Jack had found
   He kept for himself.

James Reeves

Teachers' note Ask the children to read the poems quietly to themselves and then invite two of them to read them aloud while the others listen. Ask them to tell the story of each poem. Are the stories as simple as they seem at first? In each poem, what tells them this? Discuss the different structure of each poem (see **Notes on the activities**, page 68). See also page 76.

Developing Literacy
Poetry Compendium:
Ages 7–11
© A & C BLACK

Two seaside poems: 2

- **What can you tell about the characters of the children in the seaside poems?**

Re-read the two poems.

Name	What he or she is like	How you can tell
maggie		
milly		
molly		
may		
Susan		
Sam		
Jack		

- **Write notes about three or four children, from books you have read.**
- **Imagine those children playing by the sea. What might they do? What might they find?**

What do you know about their characters?

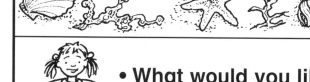

Now try this!

- **What would you like to find by the sea? Why?**

Teachers' note The children should first complete page 75. Ask them to describe what the children in both poems found by the sea. What does it tell them about the children? Ask what else the children could have found. They could list items which might be found on a beach (including rubbish).

Developing Literacy
Poetry Compendium:
Ages 7–11
© A & C BLACK

Seaside poem writer

Title	This poem is modelled on
Number of verses or stanzas	**Number of lines in each verse or stanza**

Notes on the contents of each verse or stanza

1.

2.

3.

4.

You could use some of the words from the original poem.

Useful words

bag   bone

bright   dirty

jewelled   rotting   rusty

sea anemone   sparkling

Add some of your own.

Useful rhymes

bone	bright	early	moan
stone	light	fairly	thrown
	night		
	fright		
	fight		

Now try this!

- **Write your own seaside poem.**
- **Read it aloud.**

Edit and re-draft your poem.

Teachers' note The children should first complete pages 75 and 76. Ask them to choose one of the poems from page 75 on which to model their own. The poem need not rhyme, but the children could list any useful rhymes which come to mind. They could also list any alliterative words they might use.

Developing Literacy
Poetry Compendium:
Ages 7–11
© A & C BLACK

E. E. Cummings uses punctuation and spacing to create effects.

- **Read this poem aloud.**
- **Mark the places where you paused.**

II	long pause
I	shorter pause

- **Which groups of words did you read most quickly?**
- **Write them here.**

_____

_____

_____

- **What made you read these words quickly?**

_____

_____

_____

in Just

in Just-
spring   when the world is mud-
luscious the little
lame balloonman

whistles   far   and   wee

and eddieandbill come
running from marbles and
piracies and it's
spring

when the world is puddle-wonderful

the queer
old balloonman whistles
far   and   wee
and bettyandisbel come dancing

from hop-scotch and jump-rope and

it's
spring
and
      the

         goat-footed

balloonMan   whistles
far
and
wee

E. E. Cummings

Now try this!

- **Which words in the poem seem to float into the air?**
- **Describe how the poet has done this.**

Think about spacing, alliteration and onomatopoeia.

Teachers' note The children should notice the difference between the way in which this poem is punctuated and conventional punctuation. Do they notice how the spacing of 'far   and   wee' makes the sound seem to float into the air, and how the joining up of the children's names makes the poem speed up?

Developing Literacy
Poetry Compendium:
Ages 7–11
© A & C BLACK

E. E. Cummings makes up words by joining other words. These new words have | internal rhyme | .

- Circle the internal rhyme. | mud-luscious | | puddle-wonderful |

- Choose pairs of words from below. Make up new words to describe kinds of weather. Try to use internal rhymes.

mist

lonely

ice-biting

slush

slush-mucky

wind

throttling

bitter

sun

glowing

whistling

choking

dim

snow

rain

mucky

fog

grey

biting

chilly

wondrous

ice

singing

Now try this!

- **Make up some words to describe the scene outside your school.**
- **Use internal rhyme.**
- **Think about everything which is happening: the weather, buildings, what people are doing, traffic and animals.**

Use a thesaurus.

Teachers' note The children should first complete page 78. They could draw and describe the impressions created by the words 'mud-luscious' and 'puddle-wonderful' and notice the internal rhymes (in both cases the 'u' sound). They could create other new words which include 'mud' or 'puddle' for a different effect (for example 'mud-clogged' or 'puddle-slopped').

**Developing Literacy
Poetry Compendium:
Ages 7–11
© A & C BLACK**

A poem without rhyme

This poem has no rhyme.

It has other kinds of patterns.

- **Underline examples of** [alliteration] **and** [repetition] .
  Use different colours.

alliteration _____

repetition _____

Write the colours you have used.

The Song of Life

Time passes
The sun
Burns the land
And brings about anxiety
But one day
The rainy season
Arrives
And the trees start burgeoning
The mango trees
The lemon trees
The guava trees
Give out their scents
The hibiscus flowers
Show off their beauty
The flame trees
Dance in the wind
And the whole savannah
Sings
And people
Dance
And the Mask
Dances
And the tom-tom
Beats the cadence
Of life
Which comes back
Again and again
For, people die
And people are born
People die
And people are born
Until the end
Of time.

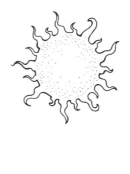

- **Count the syllables in each line. Write the total next to the start.**
- **Write down the patterns you notice.**

_____

_____

_____

_____

_____

_____

_____

_____

Véronique Tadjo

Now try this!

- **Explain what the poet is saying about life.**
  Say how the patterns in the poem help in this.

Teachers' note Introduce or revise alliteration and repetition. The children should underline each of them with a different colour and use the same colours to underline the examples they find in the poem. Ask the children to look and listen for the patterns. The children might need help in understanding the meanings of words such as 'hibiscus', 'guava', 'cadence' and 'savannah'.

Developing Literacy
Poetry Compendium:
Ages 7–11
© A & C BLACK

Free verse

The Fulani Creation Story

At the beginning there was a huge drop of milk.
Then Doondari came and he created the stone.
Then the stone created iron;
And iron created fire;
And fire created water;
And water created air.
Then Doondari descended the second time.
And he took the five elements
And he shaped them into man.
But man was proud.
Then Doondari created blindness, and blindness
defeated man.
But blindness became too proud,
Doondari created sleep, and sleep defeated blindness;
But when sleep became too proud,
Doondari created worry, and worry defeated sleep;
But when worry became too proud,
Doondari created death, and death defeated worry.
But then death became too proud,
Doondari descended for the third time,
And he came as Gueno, the eternal one.
And Gueno defeated death.

- **Does the poem** | rhyme |**?** _____

- **Count the** | syllables | **in each line.**

- **Write how many there are at the end of each line.**

- **Is there a** | pattern |**?** _____

- **Describe the pattern in the story of the poem.**

_____

_____

_____

Now try this!

- **Describe how the poem
  is different from prose.**

Think about lines and sentences.

Teachers' note To help the children to appreciate the differences between free verse and other poetry, encourage them to re-read other poems they have read (especially those with distinct rhyme patterns, rhythms and syllable patterns) and to point out any differences. They could key in the poem on this page, rearrange it as prose and explain what difference this makes.

**Developing Literacy
Poetry Compendium:
Ages 7–11
© A & C BLACK**

Two poets: research

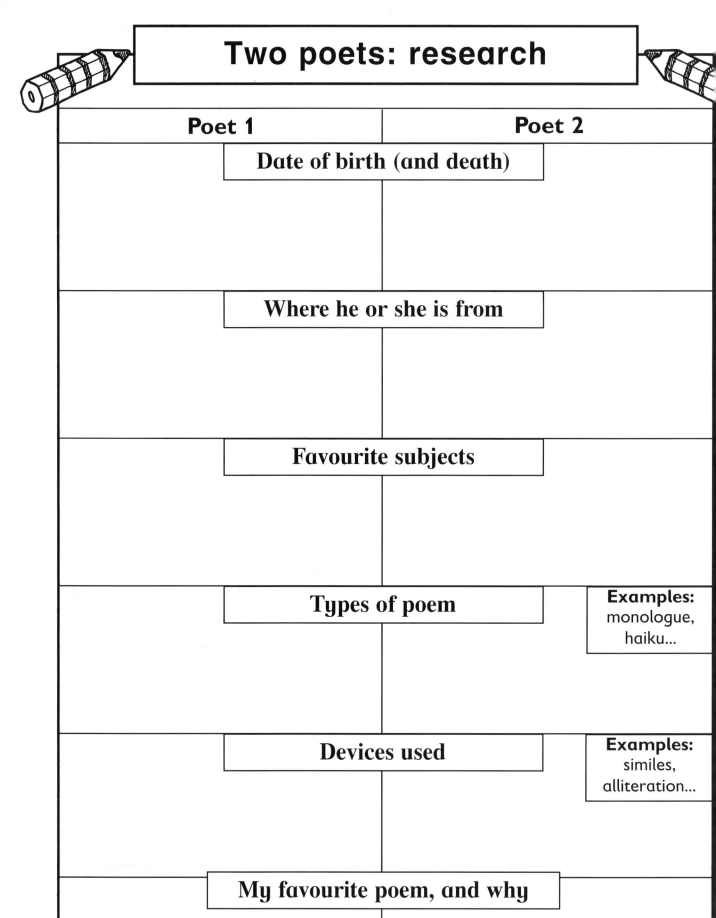

	Poet 1	Poet 2
Date of birth (and death)		
Where he or she is from		
Favourite subjects		
Types of poem		**Examples:** monologue, haiku...
Devices used		**Examples:** similes, alliteration...
My favourite poem, and why		

Teachers' note Discuss any two poets whose work the children have read, and provide information about them as well as poetry books to which the children can refer. Ask them to include in their writing anything they think is unusual about the poets' work.

Developing Literacy Poetry Compendium: Ages 7–11 © A & C BLACK

- **Read the poem aloud.**
- **Circle the** rhyming words **.**

Use a different colour for each rhyming sound.

- **Draw lines to show where the** rhyme patterns **change.**
- **How do the rhyme patterns help to link one idea in the poem to the next?**

_____
_____
_____
_____
_____
_____
_____
_____
_____

There was a naughty boy,
    And a naughty boy was he,
He ran away to Scotland
    The people for to see –
        Then he found
        That the ground
        Was as hard,
        That a yard
        Was as long,
        That a song
        Was as merry,
        That a cherry
        Was as red –
        That lead
        Was as weighty,
        That fourscore
        Was as eighty,
        That a door
        Was as wooden
        As in England –
So he stood in his shoes
    And he wonder'd,
        He wonder'd,
    He stood in his
        Shoes and he wonder'd.

from *A Song About Myself* by John Keats

Now try this!

Plan a group reading of the poem.
- **Copy and complete the chart.**

How many sections? Think about the changes in rhythm.

We can split the poem into ☐ sections.		
Section number	**Number of voices**	**Tone, speed and rhythm**

- **With your group, read the poem aloud in a way which expresses the story.**

Teachers' note Allow the children to decide how this poem should be read. Display an enlarged copy of the poem and ask the children to come out and indicate the rhyming words. To help them to describe the rhyme and rhythm patterns, they could number the lines on this enlarged copy. During the plenary session, groups could take turns to read the poem aloud.

**Developing Literacy
Poetry Compendium:
Ages 7–11
© A & C BLACK**

Travellers' tales: 1

These are the first two of the ten verses of *How They Brought the Good News from Ghent to Aix* **by Robert Browning.**

Use a dictionary.

I sprang to the stirrup, and Joris, and he;
I galloped, Dirck galloped, we galloped all three;
"Good speed!" cried the watch, as the gate-bolts undrew;
"Speed!" echoed the wall to us galloping through;
Behind shut the postern, the lights sank to rest,
And into the midnight we galloped abreast.

Not a word to each other; we kept the great pace
Neck by neck, stride by stride, never changing our place;
I turned in my saddle and made its girths tight,
Then shortened each stirrup, and set the pique right,
Rebuckled the cheek-strap, chained slacker the bit,
Nor galloped less steadily Roland a whit.

Robert Browning

This is a narrative poem **. What kind of story do you think it is?**

love ☐   tragedy ☐   adventure ☐   comedy ☐

- **What makes you think this?** _____

_____

_____

- **Describe what is happening in the poem.** _____

_____

- **What is the atmosphere of the poem?**

jolly ☐   tense ☐   sad ☐   mysterious ☐

- **What makes you think this?** _____

_____

_____

Now try this!

- **Describe how you think the speaker is feeling. Give evidence from the poem.**

Teachers' note Ask the children to read the poem silently, to picture the scene and events and to imagine how the poem should sound; invite them to share their responses. They should notice the 'galloping' rhythm and the fast pace of the poem. Provide books or tape recordings containing the poem for the children to read or listen to in its entirety.

Developing Literacy
Poetry Compendium:
Ages 7–11
© A & C BLACK

Travellers' tales: 2

- **Read this poem extract.**
- **How is it similar to** *How They Brought the Good News from Ghent to Aix***?**

Think about subject, time of day, animals, the age of the poems.

"Is there anybody there?" said the Traveller,
  Knocking on the moonlit door;
  And his horse in the silence champed the grasses
  Of the forest's ferny floor:
And a bird flew up out of the turret,
  Above the Traveller's head:
And he smote upon the door again a second time;
  "Is there anybody there?" he said.
But no one descended to the Traveller;
  No head from the leaf-fringed sill
Leaned over and looked into his grey eyes,
  Where he stood perplexed and still.
But only a host of phantom listeners
  That dwelt in the lone house then
Stood listening in the quiet of the moonlight
  To that voice from the world of men...

from *The Listeners* by Walter de la Mare

_____
_____
_____
_____
_____
_____
_____
_____

- **How are the two poems different?**

Think about atmosphere, rhythm, pace and feelings.

_____
_____
_____
_____
_____
_____
_____
_____

Now try this!

- **Write about which of the two poems you prefer, and why. Explain your answer by referring to parts of the poem.**

Teachers' note Ask the children to read the poem silently, to picture the scene and events and to imagine how the poem should sound; invite them to share their responses. Make copies of the questions on page 84, which the children can answer about both poems for comparison.

Developing Literacy Poetry Compendium: Ages 7–11 © A & C BLACK

A fox and a stag: 1

When the pods went pop on the broom, green broom,
And apples began to be golden-skinned,
We harboured a stag by the Priory coomb,
And we feathered his trail up-wind, up-wind,
We feathered his trail up-wind –
A stag of warrant*, a stag, a stag,
A runnable* stag, a kingly crop,
Brown, bay* and tray* and three on top*,
A stag, a runnable stag …

For a matter of twenty miles or more,
By the deepest hedge and the highest wall,
Through herds of bullocks he baffled the lore
Of harbourer, huntsman, hounds and all,
Of harbourer, hounds and all –
The stag of warrant, the wily stag,
For twenty miles, and five and five,
He ran, and he never was caught alive,
This stag, this runnable stag ….

Three hundred gentlemen, able to ride,
Three hundred horses as gallant and free,
Beheld him escape on the evening tide,
Far out till he sank in the Severn Sea,
Till he sank in the depths of the sea –
The stag, the buoyant stag, the stag
That slept at last in a jewelled bed
Under the sheltering ocean spread,
The stag, the runnable stag.

from *A Runnable Stag* by John Davidson

The fox was strong, he was full of running,
He could run for an hour and then be cunning,
But the cry behind him made him chill,
They were nearer now and they meant to kill.
They meant to run him until his blood
Clogged on his heart as his brush* with mud,
Till his back bent up and his tongue hung flagging
And his belly and brush were filthed from dragging
Till he crouched stone-still, dead-beat and dirty,
With nothing but teeth against the thirty.
And all the way to that blinding end
He would meet with men and have none his friend:
Men to holloa and men to run him,
With stones to stagger and yells to stun him;
Men to head him, with whips to beat him;
Teeth to mangle and mouths to eat him.
And all the way, that wild high crying,
To cold his blood with the thought of dying,
The horn and the cheer, and the drum-like thunder
Of the horse-hooves stamping the meadows under.
He upped his brush and went with a will
For the Sarsen Stones* on Wan Dyke Hill*.

from *Reynard the Fox* by John Masefield

* **of warrant** – old enough to be hunted
* **runnable** – old enough to be hunted (five or six years)
* **bay** – the second branch of an antler
* **tray** – the third branch of an antler
* **three on top** – with three branches on top of the bay and tray branches
* **brush** – a fox's tail
* **Sarsen Stones** – large standing stones used in ancient ceremonies
* **Wan Dyke Hill** (or Wansdyke) – an earthwork near Bath, built by Roman-Britons

Teachers' note Read each poem aloud to the children and ask them what is happening in each of them. Why are the fox and the stag running? From whom? What would happen to each animal if it were caught? How do the children think the hunters feel during the chase and at the end in *A Runnable Stag*? How can they tell? See also page 87.

Developing Literacy
Poetry Compendium:
Ages 7–11
© A & C BLACK

A fox and a stag: 2

- **Compare the two poems** *A Runnable Stag* **and** *Reynard the Fox*.
Support your answers with words from the poems.

Points to compare	A Runnable Stag	Reynard the Fox
Point of view		
In which person is the poem written? Why do you think this is?		
Atmosphere		
What do the opening lines make you expect of the poem?		
Of what do the rhythm and pace of the poem remind you?		
Did the animals or the hunters, or both, or neither, 'win' the chase? How can you tell?		

- **How do you feel about the animals at the beginning and end of each poem?**
- **What made you feel this? Give examples.**

Now try this!

Teachers' note Continued from page 86. During the plenary session ask the children how the first poet makes us feel we are riding with the hunters (the stag is always in the distance: 'we feathered his trail', 'for a matter of twenty miles' and 'far out'). How does the second poet make us feel we are running with the fox?

**Developing Literacy
Poetry Compendium:
Ages 7–11
© A & C BLACK**

The Charge of the Light Brigade

Half a league, half a league,
Half a league onward,
All in the valley of Death
   Rode the six hundred.
   "Forward the Light Brigade!
Charge for the guns!" he said.
Into the valley of Death
   Rode the six hundred.

"Forward the Light Brigade!"
Was there a man dismayed?
Not though the soldier knew
   Some one had blundered.
Theirs not to make reply,
Theirs not to reason why,
Theirs but to do and die.
Into the valley of Death
   Rode the six hundred.

Cannon to right of them,
Cannon to left of them,
Cannon in front of them
   Volleyed and thundered;
Stormed at with shot and shell,
Boldly they rode and well,
Into the jaws of Death,
Into the mouth of Hell
   Rode the six hundred.

Flashed all the sabres bare,
Flashed as they turned in air
Sabring the gunners there,
Charging an army, while
   All the world wondered:
Plunged in the battery-smoke
Right through the line they broke;
Cossack and Russian
Reeled from the sabre-stroke
   Shattered and sundered.
Then they rode back, but not,
   Not the six hundred.

Cannon to right of them,
Cannon to left of them,
Cannon behind them
   Volleyed and thundered;
Stormed at with shot and shell,
While horse and hero fell,
They that had fought so well
Came through the jaws of Death,
Back from the mouth of Hell,
All that was left of them,
   Left of the six hundred.

When can their glory fade?
O the wild charge they made!
   All the world wondered.
Honour the charge they made!
Honour the Light Brigade,
   Noble six hundred!

Alfred, Lord Tennyson

Teachers' note Ask the children to describe the picture which the poem creates in their imagination. They could give a summary of the story of the poem and comment on the way in which the poem's rhythm reflects the action which is happening in it. See also page 89.

Developing Literacy
Poetry Compendium:
Ages 7–11
© A & C BLACK

Speed, rhythm and rhyme: 2

- **Read** *The Charge of the Light Brigade.*

- **What do the speed and rhythm of the poem remind you of?**

_____

- **Which repeated words help to create this rhythm?**

_____

_____

_____

Think about the whole poem, rather than looking at each verse separately.

- **How do the lengths of the lines help to create speed?**

_____

_____

_____

- **Underline the rhyming words in different colours. What do you notice about the rhyme pattern?**

_____

_____

_____

_____

It will help if you number the lines first.

In verses 1 to 5 there is a change of rhythm.

- **Draw a line to show where this happens in each verse.**

- **How does the rhyme change?**

_____

Now try this!

- **Why did the poet make the change in rhythm in verses 1 to 5?**

- **What was he writing about in the first part of the verse?**

- **What was he saying in the second part?**

Think about description and opinion.

Teachers' note Use this with page 88. The children could first describe the structure of the poem: what do they notice about the lengths of the verses? They might be able to comment on the effect of this.

Developing Literacy
Poetry Compendium:
Ages 7–11
© A & C BLACK

Narrative poetry log

Which words or effects did you enjoy the most?

Title	Poet (and dates)	Type (e.g. comedy, tragedy adventure, mystery)	Personal response
How They Brought the Good News from Ghent to Aix	Robert Browning (1812 – 1898)		
The Listeners	Walter de la Mare (1873 – 1956)		

Teachers' note The children can use this page to record details of, and their personal responses to, narrative poems they have read. Set aside five minutes each day for a week during which the children can be invited to read a narrative poem aloud to the rest of the class, to say who wrote it and when, and what they like about it.

Developing Literacy Poetry Compendium: Ages 7–11
© A & C BLACK

Read it aloud

- **How should this poem be read aloud?**
- **Read the poem and complete the chart.**

Mawu of the Waters

I am Mawu of the Waters.
With mountains as my footstool
And stars in my curls
I reach down to reap the waters with my fingers
And look! I cup lakes in my palms.
I fling oceans around me like a shawl
And I am transformed
Into a waterfall.
Springs flow through me
And spill rivers at my feet
As fresh streams surge
To make seas.

Abena P. A. Busia

How to read the poem aloud (shade in the answer box)	Evidence from the poem
Number of voices 1 2 3 or more	
Tone nervous strong humorous questioning	
Speed slow fast	
Rhythm marching dancing chattering flowing	

Now try this!

- **Describe the picture you have in your mind of Mawu of the Waters. Use evidence from the poem.**
- **Practise reading the poem.**

Teachers' note Allow the children to decide how the poem should be read. The 'evidence' should explain how they chose their answers. During the plenary session individuals could take turns to read the poem aloud, and then to explain why they read it as they did: how were they trying to present Mawu?

**Developing Literacy
Poetry Compendium:
Ages 7–11
© A & C BLACK**

Rap

- **Read the** rap **aloud with your group.**
- **Quietly clap the rhythm.**

Write-A-Rap Rap

Hey, everybody, let's write a rap.
First there's a rhythm you'll need to clap.
Keep that rhythm and stay in time,
'cause a rap needs rhythm and a good strong rhyme.

The rhyme keeps coming in the very same place
so don't fall behind and try not to race.
The rhythm keeps the tap on a regular beat
and the rhyme helps to wrap your rap up neat.

'But what'll we write?' I hear you shout.
There ain't no rules for what a rap's about.
You can rap about a robber, you can rap about a king,
you can rap about a chewed up piece of string …
(well, you can rap about almost … anything!)

You can rap about the ceiling, you can rap about the floor,
you can rap about the window, write a rap on the door.
You can rap about things that are mean or pleasant,
you can rap about wrapping up a Christmas present.

You can rap about a mystery hidden in a box,
you can rap about a pair of smelly old socks.
You can rap about something that's over and gone,
you can rap about something that's going on and on and on and
on …

But when you think there just ain't nothing left to say …
you can wrap it all up and put it away.
It's a rap. It's a rap. It's a rap rap rap rap RAP!

Tony Mitton

A robber came robbing in Mum's bedroom – so she flicked him downstairs with the end of a broom…

- **In the boxes, write the number of syllables in each line.**

- **Make notes to help you to write a rap about yourself.**

Now try this!

Think about: things you like, things you say, things you do.

Teachers' note Use this with page 93. Revise syllables and encourage the children to count the syllables of each line to themselves. Also revise 'stresses' and ask them to notice where the stress falls in each line. Help them to amend the first verse so that it introduces their class. The first line could be kept as it is and the second altered, to say what the rap is about. Continued on page 93.

Developing Literacy
Poetry Compendium:
Ages 7–11
© A & C BLACK

Rap writer

• **For a class** rap **, write a verse about yourself.**

First draft

Line 1 My name's _____
and I _____

Line 2 _____
Line 3 _____
Line 4 _____
Line 5 _____
Line 6 _____
Line 7 _____
Line 8 _____

List useful rhyming words here.

• **Read your rap and clap the rhythm.**
• **Mark anything you need to change.**
• **Write your 'polished' verse.**

Use a rhyme dictionary.

My name's _____

_____

_____

_____

_____

_____

_____

Now try this!

• **With your group, write another verse to introduce your group into a class rap. You could begin like this:**

We're the group _____

We _____

Teachers' note The children should use the notes they made on page 92. There is space on this page for them to make additional notes on the words for which they need to find a rhyme. If they have written a line for which they cannot find a sensible rhyme, they should alter it. After they have written their first draft, ask them to count the syllables in each line to check the rhythm.

Developing Literacy Poetry Compendium: Ages 7–11 © A & C BLACK

A poem to perform: 1

- **Write a new verse for 'Baa, Baa Black Sheep'**
for younger children to perform.

Example:

Write a line and then check it. Follow the arrows on the flow-chart.

Cluck, cluck Red Hen,
What have you laid?
Eggs, sir, eggs, sir –
For the maid.
Fry them or boil them,
Scramble or bake,
Make an omelette,
Or even bake a cake.

Think of an animal and its sound.

Line 1

Line 2

Ask a question.

Line 3

Write the last word in line 2. _____
Think of words that rhyme with it. _____

Do the rhymes make sense?

no → Re-write Line 2 and perhaps Line 3.

yes

Line 4

Line 4 rhymes with Line 2.

Go to next page.

Teachers' note Discuss the ways in which the children could add a verse to this well-known eight-line nursery rhyme. They should follow the flow-chart, which provides space for listing rhyming words and helps the children to avoid using rhyme for its own sake if it does not make sense. Continued on page 95.

Developing Literacy
Poetry Compendium:
Ages 7–11
© A & C BLACK

A poem to perform: 2

Line 5

Line 6

Line 7

Write the last word in line 6. _____
Think of words that rhyme with it. _____

Do the rhymes make sense?

no → Re-write Line 6 and perhaps Line 7.

yes

Line 8 rhymes with Line 6.

Line 8

• Copy the chart below. Record:
– the actions the children could do
– the sound effects they could make.

You don't need an action or sound effect for <u>every</u> line.

Now try this!

Line	Actions	Sound effects

Teachers' note Continued from page 94. Different groups of children could write collaboratively about different animals: for example, a hen, a horse, a pig, a goose, a donkey, a duck or a cat. The question in Line 2 should relate to the animal's use on a farm, whether for producing food or other commodities or doing a job (like catching mice or carrying people or goods).

Developing Literacy Poetry Compendium: Ages 7–11 © A & C BLACK

Conversation poem: 1

- **Read the poem aloud with a group.**

- **Make notes on how the spoken words should sound.**

surprised, interested

The Visitor

A crumbling churchyard, the sea and the moon;
The waves had gouged out grave and bone;
A man was walking, late and alone…

He saw a skeleton on the ground;
A ring on a bony hand he found.

He ran home to his wife and gave her the ring.
"Oh, where did you get it?" He said not a thing.

"It's the prettiest ring in the world," she said,
As it glowed on her finger. They skipped off to bed.

At midnight they woke. In the dark outside–
"Give me my ring!" a chill voice cried.

"What was that, William? What did it say?"
"Don't worry, my dear. It'll soon go away."

"I'm coming!" A skeleton opened the door.
"Give me my ring!" It was crossing the floor.

"What was that, William? What did it say?"
"Don't worry, my dear. It'll soon go away."

"I'm touching you now! I'm climbing the bed."
The wife pulled the sheet right over her head.

It was torn from her grasp and tossed in the air:
"I'll drag you out of your bed by the hair!"

"What was that, William? What did it say?"
"Throw the ring through the window!
THROW IT AWAY!"

She threw it. The skeleton leapt from the sill,
Scooped up the ring and clattered downhill,
Fainter… and fainter… Then all was still.

Ian Serraillier

 • **Describe how the poet builds the tension in the poem.**

Teachers' note Read the first two verses aloud and ask the children about the atmosphere they create. Invite them to demonstrate how to read different parts of it and how to read each different voice. They could underline the words of each speaker and the narrator in different colours before reading it in their group as a dialogue.

**Developing Literacy
Poetry Compendium:
Ages 7–11
© A & C BLACK**

Conversation poem: 2

• **Plan a conversation poem to read aloud.**

What happens?

Story summary		
Setting	**Atmosphere**	**Characters**

Notes

Opening

Conversation

Ending

• **Now write your poem.**

Now try this!

• **Read your poem aloud.**
• **Make any changes which will improve it.**
• **Practise reading the final version aloud.**

Teachers' note Use this with page 96. The children could first give a brief summary of the story of 'The Visitor'. Their own conversation poem could tell a story they know. Ask them to give a brief summary of a short story the whole class knows, to identify the characters and narrator in it and to say how they would set the scene (in two verses) for this story.

Developing Literacy
Poetry Compendium:
Ages 7–11
© A & C BLACK

Notes on the activities

The notes below expand upon those provided at the bottom of the activity pages. They give ideas and suggestions for making the most of the activity sheet, including suggestions for the whole-class introduction, the plenary session or for follow-up work using an adapted version of the sheet. To help teachers to select appropriate learning experiences for their pupils, the activities are grouped into units in line with the Primary Framework for Literacy, but the pages need not be presented in the order in which they appear, unless stated otherwise.

Unit 1: The power of imagery

The activities in this section develop the children's understanding of the devices which poets use and the ways in which they convey meaning by their choice of words. It also helps the children to develop their own skills in working with imagery, rhyme, alliteration and other effects, and in selecting words to convey feelings or impressions.

A house awakes (page 102). This activity introduces personification. The children are invited to think of a house and all the things in and around it as if they were human. The introductory session or a guided writing activity could include a discussion of the sounds and actions of objects such as garage doors, locks, lights, gutters, gratings, taps, heating, plumbing, kettles and alarm clocks. They might moan, groan, complain, growl, blink, gargle, swallow, shiver or scream. The children's ideas could be read during the shared reading introduction to another lesson, leading to the writing of a class poem about a house falling asleep.

Figurative language (page 103). This poem consolidates the children's appreciation of figurative language and encourages them to explore ways in which they can enrich their own writing. Comparisons and similes: 'round as a pillow', 'whiter than milk', 'softer than if it were covered with silk', 'like men in a battle'; metaphors: 'cushion of snow', 'his claws'; personification: 'What way does he go?' 'He rides', 'his sounding flight', 'He will suddenly stop', 'he makes a pause', '[he] growls'. It is as if the wind were playing hide-and-seek with people.

Inventing words (page 104). This activity encourages the children to investigate the ways in which poets combine words in unexpected ways, sometimes linking them to make new words, and even inventing words to convey impressions. It invites the children to explore ways in which they can make up words. A good dictionary, such as *The Shorter Oxford Dictionary* (in book or CD-ROM form), should be provided. It would be helpful to explain to children who are not familiar with Scottish terms the meanings of words such as 'burn', 'brae' and 'bonny' (in 'beadbonny').

Kennings (page 105). Here the children explore poetic phrases or kennings. The activity could be linked with work on word derivations, in which they are likely to come across many words of Old Norse origin which have come from kennings. *Answers*: 11 skyscraper, 12 clothes horse, 13 gold-digger, 14 joyrider.

The unknown (page 106). The children investigate the ways in which the poet creates a feeling of fear, partly by describing parts of the Snitterjipe and evidence of his presence – the whole creature is never seen. This gives it a mysterious air. The descriptions are graphic: for example, 'his eyeballs in the dark / Shining and shifting in their sockets', 'his nostrils flaming wide', 'tapering teeth' and 'jutting jaws'. The fear and mystery are heightened by the descriptions of evidence of the Snitterjipe's presence, such as his 'sharp breath', 'hairy shadow', 'they hear him munch' and 'his fearsome prints'.

Atmosphere: 1 (page 107). In the poem 'Noon', the children learn to appreciate the ways in which poets use words to create a mood or atmosphere. *Suggested answers*: the weather is hot and humid and there is not a breath of wind (introduce the word 'oppressive'); the mood is one of sluggishness – it is too hot for movement; the bird longs for a refreshing shower of rain; the creatures are hardly moving except to try to find shady cool places. Anyone in the scene would feel hot and clammy; they would probably want to splash in cool water or rest in a shady, cool place. In the extension activity, the children should notice the contrast between the still, oppressive heat and the splashing of the bird in the cooling stream.

Atmosphere: 2 (page 108). The mood of this verse from Sir Henry Newbolt's poem 'Vitaï Lampada' (Torch of life) can be compared with that of 'Noon' (page 107). The atmosphere of this war poem is also still and quiet but, unlike in 'Noon', there is a feeling of expectation that something is about to happen. This verse is about a cricket match in which the last player is about to bat. There is a 'breathless hush' because victory depends on his performance. The poem encourages the reader to support the batting team, because it is presented from their point of view.

Rhythm and rhyme (page 109). This develops the children's ability to appreciate the effect of the rhythm and pace of a poem. The regular, smooth rhythm of this poem and its slow pace create a peaceful atmosphere which reflects the value the poet places on leisure. The children should notice that every line has eight syllables; this creates the regular rhythm. It is arranged in rhyming couplets to enhance the regularity of the rhythm.

All in a word (page 110). Here the children learn to appreciate the connotations of words. They could also write descriptions of people in which they change certain words to give different impressions: for example, smile/smirk/grin/cackle, slunk/charged/sidled/skipped, small/squat/petite, thin/slender/scrawny.

No pattern (page 111). This page provides a translation of a modern Icelandic poem. The activity develops the children's appreciation of the way in which free verse can be used to create an atmosphere and express a mood or feeling. The irregular rhythm of aimless walking reflects the subject matter – of someone wandering, without any particular purpose, through urban streets. Words which help to create the mood of loneliness are: 'emptiness', 'No life, / no sound, / not a withering leaf,' 'Nothing'.

Winter haiku (page 112). This activity consolidates the children's appreciation of the structure and essence of a haiku (see page 57) and provides a structure to help the children to write their own haiku. A haiku is unrhymed and has three lines whose syllables are arranged 5, 7, 5. Its subject is usually the natural world.

Tanka (page 113). Here the children revisit the tanka form of poetry (see page 58). A tanka has five lines. It is a haiku with two extra lines and a syllable pattern of 5, 7, 5, 7, 7. A tanka is a poem which captures the essence of a moment in time in a sustained image: for example, a bird landing on a branch, a gust of wind, someone hearing good news, a flash of lightning, or a pebble landing in a pond.

Wishing cinquains (page 114). The children revise their previous learning about cinquains (see page 59) and write their own cinquain about a wish. Encourage them to try to make up a single powerful image to express their wish, as in the example: 'Floated in the air to be caught / In nets.' Point out the syllable pattern 2, 4, 6, 8, 2. It is as if the syllable pattern stretches out and then 'snaps' back to two, like an elastic band.

What am I? (page 115). Encourage the children to think of a riddle as a series of clues which lead the reader to the answer. This activity develops their appreciation of 'play on words': for example, 'gathering of dusk'/'gathering of dust'. The extension activity invites the children to incorporate figures of speech into their own riddles.

Limerick rhyme patterns (page 116). This activity introduces the structure of the limerick, a five-line nonsense poem usually with an *aabba* rhyme scheme. The children could read other limericks by Edward Lear as well as modern limericks by poets such as John Irwin, Jack Ousbey, Judith Nicholls and Paul Cookson.

Sounds funny: 1 (page 117). In this poem, the humour depends on the similarity of sounds between words for vegetables, fruits and other plants and other words. Another poem which depends on this type of humour is 'Potato Clock' by Roger McGough in *Sky in the Pie* (Puffin). *Answers*: care at, beats, turned-up, reddish, can't elope, let us, we'd, pair; fir, plane, oak, rowan, willow, ash, leaf.

Sounds funny: 2 (page 118). This activity introduces the humour of 'spoonerisms' and encourages the children to make up some of their own. A modern poem which makes use of 'spoonerisms' is 'Here is the Feather Warcast' by Trevor Millum, in *Read Me: A Poem a Day for the National Year of Reading* (Macmillan). *Answers*: 1 poured with rain, 2 stuck in the mud, 3 keen as mustard, 4 reading books, 5 dogs lie, 6 square meals. *Shopping list*: a mound of peat, a pan of cares, a bin of teens, bellyjeans, keys and parrots, fates and digs, pick cheese, fleet wakes.

Playing with meanings (page 119). Encourage the children to explore the creation of humour through word association and similar-sounding words. Note that the title of the poem is a play on words (a case could contain fish; it is also an action in court). *Answers*: 'battery' is the crime of harming someone physically, fish are 'battered'; monkfish is a fish and a monk is a member of a religious order; 'cod' sounds like 'God', 'So help me God' is an oath sworn in court; soles are fish, 'souls' are people (explain the figure of speech 'lost souls'); 'crabby' means bad-tempered, crabs are sea-creatures; plaice is a fish and sounds like 'place'; whiting is a fish and sounds similar to 'writing'; skate is a fish, 'bored' sounds like 'board': the words go together to make 'skateboard'; scampi are shellfish and start with a similar sound to 'scamper'; congers are eels, congas are dances; 'wrapped up' means 'completed', fish are sold wrapped up in newspaper; Krayfish (crayfish) are shellfish and the Kray twins were notorious criminals.

An Elizabethan poem (page 120). Here the children explore the original language of an Elizabethan poem. Reading it aloud and listening carefully to the words should help them to work out what they mean. The activity develops reading skills: inferring meaning by considering syntax and context. *Answers:* 'Mutabilitie' means an ability to change. Changed spellings: 'plentious' (plenteous), 'banisht' (banished), 'eares' (ears), 'corne' (corn), 'holde' (hold), 'reape' (reap), 'Faerie' (fairy). Words used differently or no longer used: 'full' (very), 'to-fore' (until then), 'oft' (often), 'enrold' (rolled), 'yold' (yielded). Past tenses: 'banisht' (banished), 'enrold' (rolled), 'yold' (yielded). Different word-order: 'oft him pinched sore', 'he did holde'.

Unit 2: Finding a voice

The children explore poems with underlying meaning and develop their own skills in using imagery and poetic form to express a personal point of view.

Word-play (page 121). This very short poem (just one sentence) uses the homophones 'saw'/'soar'/'sore' to express an idea about a tall building. It also plays on the ambiguity of 'eyesore' (a sore eye or an ugly sight).

Comparison poem (page 122). This activity is about the images created by comparing one thing with another. Discuss what is meant by 'a man of words and not of deeds', model the first example and invite the children to complete the second and third examples as a shared writing activity. There are no 'right answers', but the following might be useful: is like a twig without a leaf; is like a sofa with soft cushions; is like a rose with extra thorns; is like a bat with the eyes of a hawk; is like a bell with the sweetest chimes.

Analysing a poem (page 123). This poem is written from the point of view of a cat observing Christmas preparations. The humour arises from the questioning of popular Christmas rituals, which sound ridiculous as observed by the cat but, in fact, are exactly what happens in many homes.

Layers of meaning (page 124). 'In This City' is a challenging poem which has a literal meaning and a deeper meaning: the woman is sad because someone switched off the light in a room, not noticing her presence. The person does not notice her existence – she feels neglected. Another poem which could be studied in the same way is 'Not Waving but Drowning' by Stevie Smith (in many anthologies, including *The*

Nation's Favourite Poems, BBC): the man drowns because people ignore him, thinking he is waving and fooling about in the water. People ignored him all his life because he was unable to communicate with them.

A poet's style (page 125). This page provides a framework to support the children's analysis of a poet's views and style. They could compare two poets: one modern and one from the past.

Native American poem (page 126). The poem 'Alabama' was written by a nineteenth-century Native American, who expresses his feelings about the loss of the land where his people used to live. The children are invited to tell the story of Khe-Tha-A-Hi's people. The poem tells a little about the culture of these people – their way of life and their outlook on life. The children might notice the sad irony that the state of Alabama bears the name given to it by the very people who were driven out of it. Native American poems can be found in *Read Me: A Poem a Day for the National Year of Reading*, *Read Me 2: A Poem for Every Day of the Year* (both Macmillan) and *Classic Poems to Read Aloud* (Puffin).

The poet's experience (page 127). This poem is from Djibouti, in Africa, from which the children can deduce a great deal about the poet's experience. They should notice that he lives in a hot, dry place ('aloe', 'cactus', 'river there is none', 'desert', 'camels' and 'dust'). Draw the children's attention to the very few possessions the poet owns (and that all of them are essential, such as camels and shoes). The last line of the poem could be discussed in contrast with the lives of most people in developed countries: it is a simple life in which, as stated in lines 8 and  9, the main preoccupation is survival. The children might also notice the feeling of vast open space which is conveyed by the words 'basaltic universe in the desert' and 'unchanging horizon'.

Your experience (page 128). The children could compare their own lifestyles with that of the nomadic child in the poem on page 127. Encourage them to think about the landscape (or cityscape) which they see around them every day, the objects which surround them and the things which preoccupy them.

Learning objectives

The following chart shows how the Ages 10–11 activity sheets (pages 102–128) match the learning objectives addressed by the Year 6 units in the Poetry block of the Primary Framework for Literacy. (Where a page number is shown in bold type, this indicates the learning objective is the main focus of the activity.)

Objectives	Unit 1: The power of imagery	Unit 2: Finding a voice
Understanding and interpreting texts		
Understand underlying themes, causes and points of view	107–109	121, 122, **123**, **124**, 125–127
Understand how writers use different structures to create coherence and impact	102, **103**, 104, 105, **106**, **107**, **108**, **109**, 110, **111**, 112, 113, 114, **115**, 116–119	**121**, **122**, 123, 124, **125**
Engaging with and responding to texts		
Compare how writers from different times and places present experiences and use language	**104**, 105, 107, 108, **120**	121, **126**, **127**, 128
Creating and shaping texts		
Select words and language drawing on their knowledge of literary features and formal and informal writing	**102**, **105**, **110**, 112–115, **116**, **117**, **118**, **119**	121–123, 124, 127, **128**
Text structure and organisation		
Use varied structures to shape and organise texts coherently	102, **112**, **113**, **114**, 115–117	
Presentation		
Select from a wide range of ICT programs to present text effectively and communicate information and ideas	102, 103, 114	128

A house awakes

- **List the events which happen in and around a house in the morning.**

- **Write words and phrases to** personify **the house.**

Events	Personification	Useful words
curtains drawn back	windows open their eyes	arms blink cough dozing feet gargle groan hunched lazy mouth nose nosy rise shivering sing sneeze snore stare swallow teeth throat tongue wave

- **Use your notes to type out a list poem about a house in the morning. Use personification.**

- **List the events of a house at night.**
- **Personify the events.**

Teachers' note Introduce personification by reading poems which personify non-living things: for example, 'December' by Robert Southey, 'The Wind Tapped Like a Tired Man' by Emily Dickinson, 'City Jungle' by Pie Corbett, 'The Wind in a Frolic' by William Howitt, 'Your Friend the Sun' by Roger McGough or 'The Wind and the Moon' by George MacDonald.

Developing Literacy
Poetry Compendium:
Ages 7–11
© A & C BLACK

Figurative language

This poem uses figurative language **– similes and comparisons, metaphors and personification.**

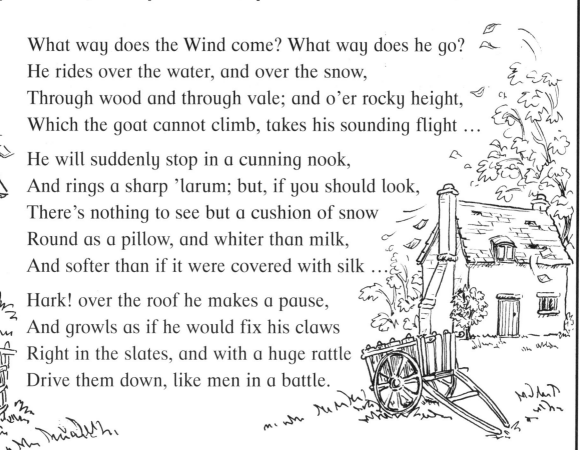

What way does the Wind come? What way does he go?
He rides over the water, and over the snow,
Through wood and through vale; and o'er rocky height,
Which the goat cannot climb, takes his sounding flight …

He will suddenly stop in a cunning nook,
And rings a sharp 'larum; but, if you should look,
There's nothing to see but a cushion of snow
Round as a pillow, and whiter than milk,
And softer than if it were covered with silk …

Hark! over the roof he makes a pause,
And growls as if he would fix his claws
Right in the slates, and with a huge rattle
Drive them down, like men in a battle.

from *Address to a Child during a Boisterous Winter Evening* by Dorothy Wordsworth

• Fill in a chart like this using examples from the poem.

Similes and comparisons	Metaphors	Personification

Now try this!

• **How does the poet describe the character of the wind in each verse?**

Explain your answer using words from the poem.

Teachers' note The children will probably need to revise simile and metaphor (and, if they have not recently completed page 102, personification). Show them how to use a computer to create a chart or table for this activity.

**Developing Literacy
Poetry Compendium:
Ages 7–11
© A & C BLACK**

Inventing words

Gerard Manley Hopkins made up words in his poems and combined words in new ways.

Inversnaid

This darksome burn, horseback brown,
His rollrock highroad roaring down,
In coop and in comb the fleece of his foam
Flutes and low to the lake falls home.

A windpuff-bonnet of fawn-froth
Turns and twindles over the broth
Of a pool so pitchblack, fell-frowning,
It rounds and rounds Despair to drowning.

Degged with dew, dappled with dew
Are the groins of the braes that the brook treads through,
Wiry heathpacks, flitches of fern,
And the beadbonny ash that sits over the burn.

What would the world be, once bereft
Of wet and of wildness? Let them be left,
O let them be left, wildness and wet;
Long live the weeds and the wilderness yet.

Gerard Manley Hopkins

- **Underline any words whose meaning you do not know.**
- **Look up these words in a dictionary. Write the meanings of those you can find.**

Use a dictionary.

- **Copy and complete the chart.**

Words made by combining words		Words used in new ways		Invented words	
Word	Meaning	Word	Meaning	Word	Meaning

- **Write about a place you know.**
  Use some of your own made-up words.

Teachers' note Discuss some of the words the children might not have met before, such as 'darksome': what do they think it means? What impression do they have of Inversnaid? They should notice the wetness, thick undergrowth of ferns and heather and the wildness. Ask what the poet is saying about wild, uncultivated areas like Inversnaid.

Developing Literacy Poetry Compendium: Ages 7–11 © A & C BLACK

Kennings

Kenning is an old Norse term. It is a poetic phrase that is used instead of the name for something.

'husband' is from 'hus-bondi' (house farmer)

'mole' is from 'molde-warp' (earth thrower)

• **Write the kennings next to their meanings.**

1. battle _____

2. body _____

3. dragon _____

4. king _____

5. sea _____

6. ship _____

7. sun _____

8. vocabulary _____

9. underground den or lair _____

10. army of brave warriors _____

Kennings

bone-house	earth-hall
fire-lizard	fish-home
hero-train	ring-giver
sword-storm	wave-swimmer
word-hoard	world-candle

• **Write the modern kennings which mean:**

11. a very tall building

    s_____

12. a frame on which clothes are dried

    c_____ h_____

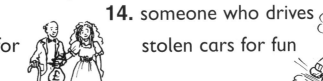

13. a person who marries someone for his or her money

    g____-d_____

14. someone who drives stolen cars for fun

    j_____

• **Make up four other kennings. Give them to a friend to work out their meanings.**

Teachers' note Give examples of poetic kennings: for example, 'wave-steed' for 'ship' and 'battle-light' for 'sword', and explain that poets used kennings to express ideas and feelings and not just to describe things or make up names for them. You could read parts of the poem *Beowulf*, pointing out the many different kennings used to refer to Beowulf himself.

Developing Literacy
Poetry Compendium:
Ages 7–11
© A & C BLACK

The unknown

The boys in the poem do not see the Snitterjipe properly.

- **Which parts of it do they see?**

_____

_____

_____

_____

- **What do they feel?**

_____

_____

- **What do they hear?**

_____

_____

- **What feeling is created in the poem?**

_____

- **List the words which create this feeling.**

_____

_____

_____

_____

_____

_____

The Snitterjipe

In mellow orchards, rich and ripe,
Is found the luminous Snitterjipe.
Bad boys who climb the bulging trees
Feel his sharp breath about their knees;
His trembling whiskers tickle so,
They squeak and squeak till they let go.
They hear his far-from-friendly bark;
They see his eyeballs in the dark
Shining and shifting in their sockets
As round and as big as pears in pockets.
They feel his hot and wrinkly hide;
They see his nostrils flaming wide,
His tapering teeth, his jutting jaws,
His tongue, his tail, his twenty claws.
His hairy shadow in the moon,
It makes them sweat, it makes them swoon;
And as they climb the orchard wall
They let their pilfered apples fall.
The Snitterjipe suspends pursuit
And falls upon the fallen fruit;
And while they flee the monster fierce,
Apples, not boys, his talons pierce.
With thumping hearts they hear him munch –
Six apples at a time he'll crunch.
At length he falls asleep, and they
On tiptoe take their homeward way.
But long before the blackbirds pipe
To welcome the day, the Snitterjipe
Has fled afar, and on the green
Only his fearsome prints are seen.

James Reeves

- **Explain how the poet makes the Snitterjipe seem mysterious.**

Teachers' note Before reading the poem ask the children what 'The Snitterjipe' might be. Do they expect the poem to be funny or serious? Why? After reading the poem ask them if their predictions were right. Note that nonsense words are used not to create humour but to create an air of mystery: no one knows what the Snitterjipe is.

**Developing Literacy
Poetry Compendium:
Ages 7–11**
© A & C BLACK

• **Describe the impressions the poet creates. Write in the boxes.**

What is the weather like ?	What is the mood?

Noon

The midday hour of twelve the clock counts o'er,
    A sultry stillness lulls the air asleep;
The very buzz of flies is heard no more,
    Nor faintest wrinkles o'er the waters creep.
Like one large sheet of glass the pool does shine,
    Reflecting in its face the burnt sunbeam:
The very fish their sturting* play decline,
    Seeking the willow shadows 'side the stream.
And, where the hawthorn branches o'er the pool,
    The little bird, forsaking song and nest,
Flutters on dripping twigs his limbs to cool,
    And splashes in the stream his burning breast.
Oh, free from thunder, for a sudden shower,
    To cherish nature in this noonday hour!

John Clare

What does the bird long for?

What are all the creatures of the pool doing?

* **sturting** – attacking, darting about

• **Describe what your body would feel like if you were in the place in the poem.** _____

_____

• **What would you feel like doing, and why?**

_____

Now try this!

• **Explain the contrast which emphasises the oppressive heat described in the poem.**

Teachers' note Read the poem aloud and ask the children what season and what time of day are being described. Is the atmosphere lively or still, fresh or sluggish? How can they tell? Model the answer to the first question, discussing the connotations of words such as 'sultry' and 'lulls' and the mood created by the alliteration in 'sultry stillness'.

Developing Literacy
Poetry Compendium:
Ages 7–11
© A & C BLACK

• **What kind of atmosphere does the first line of the poem create?**

_____

_____

_____

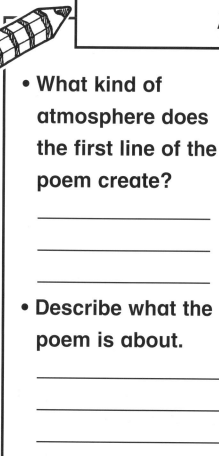

Vitaï Lampada

There's a breathless hush in the Close tonight –
Ten to make and the match to win –
A bumping pitch and a blinding light,
An hour to play and the last man in.
And it's not for the sake of a ribboned coat,
Or the selfish hope of a season's fame,
But his Captain's hand on his shoulder smote –
"Play up! play up! and play the game!"

Henry Newbolt

• **Describe what the poem is about.**

_____

_____

_____

_____

What has been going on and what is about to happen?

• **Explain why there is a 'breathless hush'.**

_____

_____

_____

• **How do you feel by the end of the poem, and why?**

Think of the atmosphere which has been built up.

_____

_____

_____

• **What do you hope will happen?**

_____

• **Make up a poem about a sport you have watched. Create as much suspense as you can.**

Teachers' note The children should first have completed page 107. Ask them what similarities they notice between the atmospheres of this and 'Noon'. What differences are there? In which poem is there a feeling that something is about to happen? Which words create this feeling? Point out the air of expectation created by the words 'breathless hush'.

Developing Literacy Poetry Compendium: Ages 7–11 © A & C BLACK

Rhythm and rhyme

- **Tick <u>all</u> the words which describe the poem.**

Speed
slow	☐
fast	☐

Rhythm
smooth	☐
jerky	☐
ambling	☐
running	☐
skipping	☐
galloping	☐

Atmosphere
peaceful	☐
aggressive	☐
tense	☐
exciting	☐

Leisure

What is this life if, full of care, ☐
We have no time to stand and stare. ☐

No time to stand beneath the boughs ☐
And stare as long as sheep or cows. ☐

No time to see, when woods we pass, ☐
Where squirrels hide their nuts in grass. ☐

No time to see, in broad daylight, ☐
Streams full of stars like skies at night. ☐

No time to turn at Beauty's glance, ☐
And watch her feet, how they can dance. ☐

No time to wait till her mouth can ☐
Enrich that smile her eyes began. ☐

A poor life this if, full of care, ☐
We have no time to stand and stare. ☐

W. H. Davies

- **Write the number of syllables in each line in the boxes.**
- **What do you notice?** _____
- **Underline the rhymes in different colours.**
  What do you notice? _____

Now try this!

- **How do the speed, rhythm and rhyme of the poem help to communicate its message?**

Teachers' note Ask the children to read the poem silently. Invite one of them to read it aloud while the others listen and comment on whether the speed and rhythm match the way in which they think it should be read. Discuss the ways in which the speed and rhythm of the poem reflect its subject. Ask the children what the poem's message is.

Developing Literacy
Poetry Compendium:
Ages 7–11
© A & C BLACK

All in a word

Well-chosen words can influence people's impressions of a person, thing, place or topic.

• Choose words from the notepad to create an impression of the word on each shape.

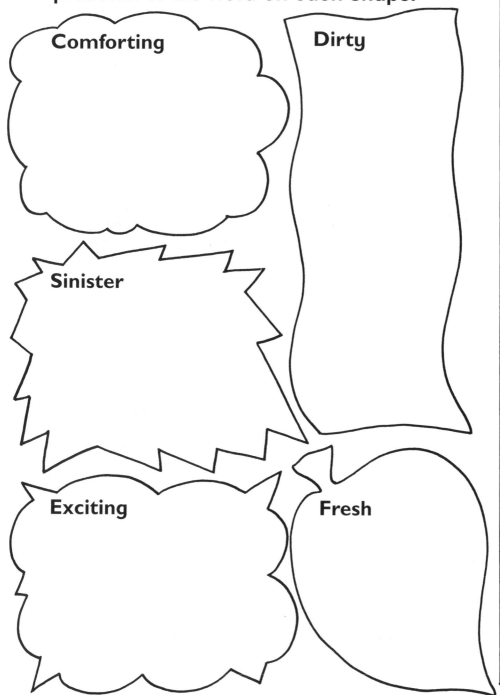

Comforting

Dirty

Sinister

Exciting

Fresh

Now try this!

• Use some of the words to write about a character.
• Change the words to create a different character.

Teachers' note Model the first example. Ask the children in which shape it should be written.
Ask them to explain their answers: what image does the word conjure up?

Developing Literacy
Poetry Compendium:
Ages 7–11
© A & C BLACK

No pattern

Free verse does not follow any pattern of rhyme, rhythm or verse structure.

Song of the Street

In brick-grey emptiness
under the moon's sickle
I walk.
No life,
no sound,
not a withering leaf,
not a flickering straw.
Nothing
but I
in brick-grey emptiness
under the moon's sickle.
And nothing exists but me.

Steinn Steinarr
(translated by Sigurour A. Magnússon)

• **Look for rhyme in the poem. What do you notice?**

_____

_____

• **Listen to the rhythm of the poem. What movement is it like?**

_____

• **What is the person in the poem doing?**

_____

• **Explain how the rhythm reflects what he is doing.**

_____

_____

• **List the negative words in the poem.**

_____

• **Describe the effect of these words.**

_____

_____

_____

Now try this!

• **Describe the mood the poet creates. Give evidence from the poem.**

Teachers' note The children will notice that there is no rhyme in the poem and, although its rhythm is neither repetitive nor regular, it is nonetheless a discernible rhythm. The children could tap this rhythm on a table-top as they read the poem silently. Ask them what it brings to mind.

Developing Literacy Poetry Compendium: Ages 7–11 © A & C BLACK

Winter haiku

- **Read the** `haiku`.

Ice on the front step –
two men slip as they bring in
a new fridge freezer.

Patricia V. Dawson

→ the scene

→ what happens and when

- **Count the syllables.**

Line 1	Line 2	Line 3	Total

A haiku is usually about nature. What is described in this haiku? _____

_____

- **Make up your own haiku.**
  The first line has been completed.

Write each syllable in a separate box.

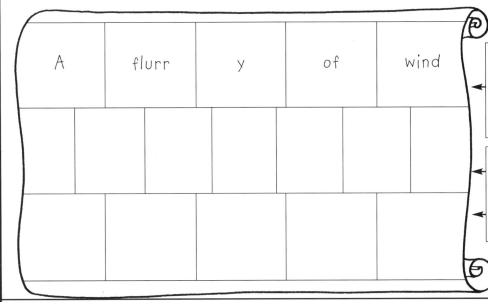

A	flurr	y	of	wind

→ the scene (something to do with nature)

→ what happens and when, where, why or how

Now try this!

- **Make up a haiku for each season of the year.**

Jot down some ideas first.

Teachers' note Revise syllables. Encourage the children to read other haiku and to count the syllables in each line. They should make jottings about what might happen in a flurry of wind, use a thesaurus to find alternative descriptive words and try out and adjust their ideas until they have the right number of syllables in each line.

**Developing Literacy
Poetry Compendium:
Ages 7–11
© A & C BLACK**

Tanka

A tanka usually describes a special moment in time. It has a set pattern.

- Count the syllables.

Line 1	Line 2	Line 3	Line 4	Line 5

Silver Aeroplane

Silver aeroplane
Speeds across the summer sky
Leaving in its wake
Trails of vapour: white scribblings
On a page of blue paper.

John Foster

- List six subjects for tankas.

1. _____
2. _____
3. _____
4. _____
5. _____
6. _____

The subjects might happen again and again, but they'll never be identical: like a rainbow, or a cat leaping onto a high wall.

- Make notes about something you have observed which would be a good subject for a tanka.

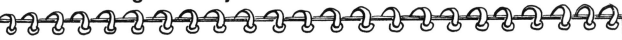

Think of comparisons, similes, metaphors and figurative language.

- Use your notes to write a tanka.

Now try this!

_____
_____
_____
_____

Teachers' note Read the poem aloud to the children before providing them with a copy of it, and ask them if they know what kind of poem it is. It might be useful to revise the structure of the tanka. Discuss the nature of the subject matter, pointing out that the trail of an aeroplane is something which lasts only a short time.

Developing Literacy
Poetry Compendium:
Ages 7–11
© A & C BLACK

Wishing cinquains

- **Read the** cinquain .
- **List three wishes of your own.**

    1. _____

    _____

    2. _____

    _____

    3. _____

    _____

I wish

I wish
The answers to
Maths questions and spellings
Floated in the air to be caught
In nets.

36 x 6 = 216 receipt

- **Plan a cinquain about one of your wishes.**

Make notes about your ideas.

- **Write your cinquain here.**

    1. _____ [2]

    2. _____ [4]

    3. _____ [6]

    4. _____ [8]

    5. _____ [2]

Check that each line has the correct number of syllables.

- **Edit and revise your cinquain.**
- **Make a 'polished' copy for a class anthology.**

Now try this!

Teachers' note Read the cinquain aloud and then ask the children to read it silently, counting the syllables in each line. Ask them what they notice about the structure and rhythm, and point out that cinquains do not usually rhyme. The children could use word-processing software to edit and 'polish' their cinquains in the extension activity.

Developing Literacy
Poetry Compendium:
Ages 7–11
© A & C BLACK

What am I?

- **Read the** riddle .
- **What is the answer?**

I am the Shame beneath a Carpet

I am the shame beneath a carpet.
No one comes to sweep me off my feet.

Abandoned rooms and unread books collect me.
Sometimes I dance like particles of light.

My legions thicken on each window pane,
A gathering of dusk, perpetual gloom,

And when at last the house has fallen,
I am the cloud left hanging in the air.

John Mole

- **In verse 3, which word is almost the same as the answer?**

- **Explain the play on meanings in the underlined words.**

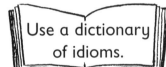

Use a dictionary of idioms.

- **Circle the** idioms **in verses 1 and 4.**

- **Match the titles of these riddle poems to their subjects. Write the answers on the chart.**

1. *I am Lost in a Haystack.*

2. *I am the Old Idea Blown Away.*

3. *I am the Material of a Hard Heart.*

4. *I am the Humiliation Left on a Face.*

a. egg

b. cobweb

c. stone

d. needle

Title	Subject
1	
2	
3	
4	

Now try this!

- **Make notes for your own riddle poem about an everyday item. Write clues to help the reader to work out the answer.**

Try to use idioms in your poem.

Teachers' note Introduce the activity by reading other riddles with the children. Ask the children what they notice about the structure of a riddle and in which person it is usually written. They will need access to a dictionary of idioms: for example, *The Penguin Dictionary of English Idioms.*

Developing Literacy Poetry Compendium: Ages 7–11 © A & C BLACK

Limerick rhyme patterns

- **Underline the** | rhymes | **in** | red |.
- **Underline** | repeated words | **in** | blue |.

These | limericks | are by Edward Lear.

There was an Old Person of Dutton
Whose head was as small as a button,
   So, to make it look big,
   He purchased a wig,
And rapidly rushed about Dutton.

There was a Young Girl of Majorca,
Whose aunt was a very fast walker;
   She walked seventy miles,
   And leaped fifteen stiles,
Which astonished that Girl of Majorca.

- **Fill in the gaps in these limericks.**

There was an Old Man of Torquay
Who spent ten pounds on a _____
He _____
_____
_____

There was a Young Lady from France
_____
_____
_____
_____

Useful rhyming words

away	day
flea	CD
tree	me
night	right
fight	light
dance	prance
chance	ease
knees	please
jig	wig

Now try this!

- **List four places and four words which rhyme with them. Use your words to make other limericks.**

Teachers' note The children could prepare for this activity by bringing in examples of limericks. Ask them how they can distinguish a limerick from any other kind of poem and discuss the number of lines, the rhythm and the rhyme pattern.

Developing Literacy
Poetry Compendium:
Ages 7–11
© A & C BLACK

Sounds funny: 1

- **Circle the names of vegetables, fruits and other plants in this poem. In the outlines, write the words they have replaced.**

care at

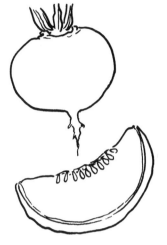

The Greengrocer's Love Song
Do you (carrot) all for me?
My heart beets for you.
With your turnip nose
And your radish face
You are a peach.
If we canteloupe
Lettuce marry.
Weed make a swell pear.

Anonymous

- **Replace each word in bold type with a word from the notepad.**

The words should have similar sounds.

Tree school playtime

"It's not **fair** (_____)!
I'm not **playing** (_____)!"
"**OK** (_____), bring your **own** (_____) ball!"
"**Will you** (_____) play with me?"
"Well, I'll **ask** (_____) my friend to join us.
"We shouldn't **leave** (_____) her out."

Useful words

ash	fir
leaf	oak
plane	rowan
willow	

Now try this!

- **Write the names of foods which sound like other words.**

  Example: pizza (piece of)
- **Use them in a poem.**

Teachers' note The activity could be introduced by reading the poem aloud to the children before they have been given a copy of it. Ask them what makes it a *greengrocer's* love song. Provide them with copies of the poem and ask them if seeing the poem in writing helps them to appreciate the humour.

Developing Literacy
Poetry Compendium:
Ages 7–11
© A & C BLACK

Sounds funny: 2

In a [spoonerism] the first letters of words are swapped. It is named after the Reverend William Spooner, who often mixed up words in this way.

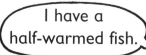

I have a half-warmed fish.

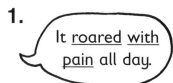

He means a half-formed wish.

• **Write the meanings of these spoonerisms.**

1. It <u>roared</u> <u>with</u> <u>pain</u> all day.

2. We were <u>muck</u> <u>in</u> <u>the</u> <u>stud</u>.

3. He's as <u>mean</u> <u>as</u> <u>custard</u>.

4. My hobby is <u>beading</u> <u>rooks</u>.

5. Let sleeping <u>logs</u> <u>die</u>.

6. He had three <u>mare</u> <u>squeals</u> per day.

1.	2.	3.
4.	5.	6.

• **Make up spoonerisms for the items on the shopping list.**

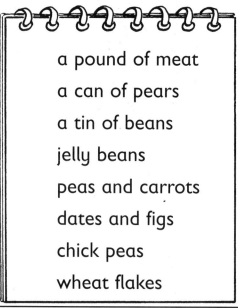

a pound of meat

a can of pears

a tin of beans

jelly beans

peas and carrots

dates and figs

chick peas

wheat flakes

Now try this!

• **Make up six spoonerisms about sports and games.**

Teachers' note Read the introduction to the activity to the children, and ask them if they have heard any examples of 'spoonerisms'. Tell them others of the Reverend Spooner's examples: 'a well-boiled icicle' and 'a boiled sprat' and ask them if they can work out what he meant to say ('a well-oiled bicycle' and 'a spoiled brat').

Developing Literacy
Poetry Compendium:
Ages 7–11
© A & C BLACK

Playing with meanings

- **Explain the humour of the words in bold type.**

Think of similar-sounding words, homophones and linked meanings.

A Bad Case of Fish

A **chip**-shop owner's in the **dock**
on a charge of assault and **battery**.
The **monkfish** takes the oath:
So help me **cod** …

The courtroom's packed with lost **soles**.
The **crabby** judge can't find his **plaice**
or read the prosecution's **whiting**.
And what sort of fish is a saveloy, anyway?

The young **skates** are getting bored.
They start **skateboarding** down the aisles.
The **scampi** scamper to and fro.
The eels are dancing **congers**.

But the case is cut and dried.
It's all **wrapped up**. (Just look
in the evening paper.) Next,
the **Krayfish twins** …

Philip Gross

Chip sounds similar to ship.

Battery means harming someone physically and fish are battered before they are cooked.

Crabby

Plaice

Whiting

Scampi

Congers

Wrapped up

Ships are found in docks. The **dock** is where witnesses give evidence in court.

Monkfish is a

Cod sounds like

Soles

Skate

Krayfish twins
Crayfish are shellfish and the Kray twins were notorious criminals.

Teachers' note Introduce different types of word-play using the names of animals: for example, 'the cows cowered' and 'the mare coughed hoarsely'. Read the poem aloud and help the children to find the word-play in the first verse. As an extension activity the children could make up other word-plays.

Developing Literacy
Poetry Compendium:
Ages 7–11
© A & C BLACK

119

An Elizabethan poem

This poem was written in Elizabethan times. Read the poem aloud. Try to work out the meanings of unfamiliar words.

What modern words do the old words sound like?

Then came the *Autumne* all in yellow clad,
As though he joyed in his plentious store,
Laden with fruits that made him laugh, full glad
That he had banisht hunger, which to-fore
Had by the belly oft him pinched sore.
Upon his head a wreath that was enrold
With eares of corne of every sort he bore:
And in his hand a sickle he did holde,
To reape the ripened fruits the which the earth had yold.

from 'Mutabilitie', part of *The Faerie Queene* by Edmund Spenser

Find out what 'Mutabilitie' means.

● **Fill in the chart.**

Elizabethan language			
Changed spellings		**Words used differently or no longer used**	
Word	Meaning	Word	Meaning
Autumne	Autumn	joyed in	enjoyed

Now try this!

● **Give examples of past tenses used in the poem which were formed differently.**
● **Write them in modern English.**
● **Give two examples of word-order which are different from modern English. Explain the differences.**

Teachers' note Read the poem aloud and ask the children to identify the subject-matter. Ask them to give a brief summary of how the poet depicts autumn. They could also comment on the use of comparison, metaphor, figurative language and personification. Encourage them to work out the meanings of the unfamiliar words from their contexts.

Developing Literacy Poetry Compendium: Ages 7–11 © A & C BLACK

Word-play

The word-play of this poem uses
three | homophones | .

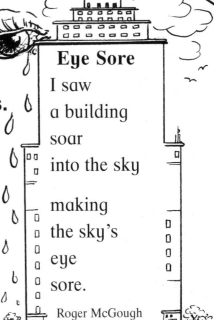

Eye Sore

I saw

a building

soar

into the sky

making

the sky's

eye

sore.

Roger McGough

- **List the homophones and their meanings.**

  1. _____ _____
     _____

  2. _____ _____
     _____

  3. _____ _____
     _____

- **What two meanings does the title of the poem have?**

  1. _____

  2. _____

- **What is the poet saying about this building (and perhaps about others)?**

  _____

Now try this!

- **Write the meanings of the homophones below.**

right	stair	fair	praise
rite	stare	fare	prays
write	stir	fir	preys

vain	road	poor	rain
vane	rode	pore	reign
vein	rowed	pour	rein

- **Write sentences to link each set of homophones.**

  Example: It was her **right** to **write** about the **rite**.

Teachers' note Introduce the activity by reading other poems which feature word-play, especially by Roger McGough, Michael Rosen and Brian Patten. For the extension activity, encourage the children to make notes of any ideas they have about links between the homophones and to talk to a partner about their ideas.

Developing Literacy
Poetry Compendium:
Ages 7–11
© A & C BLACK

Comparison poem

- **Write your own 'man of words'** comparisons .

A Man of Words

A man of words and not of deeds

A man of words and not of deeds
Is like a garden full of weeds;
And when the weeds begin to grow,
It's like a garden full of snow;
And when the snow begins to fall,
It's like a bird upon the wall;
And when the bird away does fly,
It's like an eagle in the sky;
And when the sky begins to roar,
It's like a lion at the door;
And when the door begins to crack,
It's like a stick across your back;
And when your back begins to smart,
It's like a penknife in your heart;
And when your heart begins to bleed,
You're dead, and dead, and dead indeed.

Is like a book which

Is like

Is like

Anonymous

- **Complete these comparisons.**

Your comparisons don't need to rhyme.

A person of lies and not of truth

Is like _____

A friend who comforts you when you're sad

Is like _____

Someone who gossips behind your back

Is like _____

Someone who helps you to find lost things

Is like _____

The person who calls when you think you've no friends

Is like _____

Now try this!

- **Write four other comparisons about types of people.**

Teachers' note During the introductory session read poems which contain comparisons: for example, 'Timothy Winters' by Charles Causley, 'Symphony in Yellow' by Oscar Wilde, 'Old Smoothing Iron' by Seamus Heaney and 'Autumn Birds' by John Clare. Discuss the choice of comparisons, noting how they suit the feeling or idea expressed.

Developing Literacy Poetry Compendium: Ages 7–11 © A & C BLACK

Analysing a poem

- **What is the subject of this poem?**

  _____

- **Which words tell you this?** _____

  _____

  _____

  _____

  _____

- **Does the cat understand what is going on?**

  _____

- **How can you tell?**

  _____

  _____

  _____

  _____

  _____

  _____

  _____

  _____

  _____

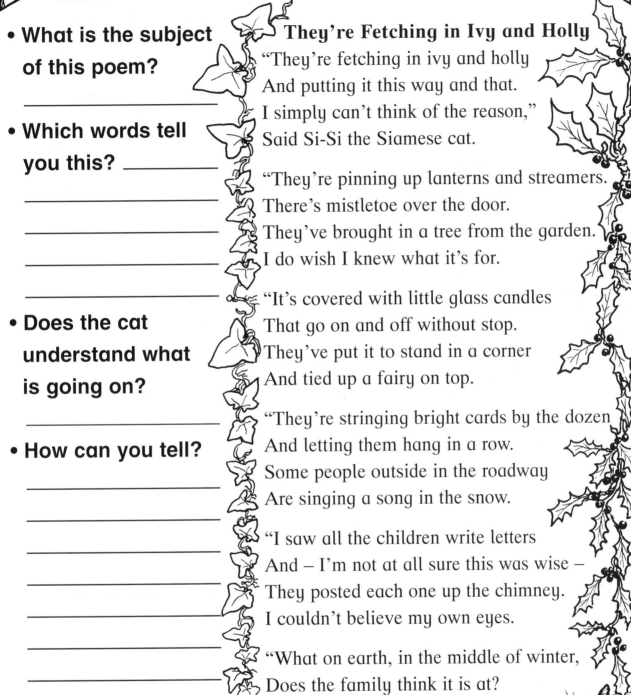

They're Fetching in Ivy and Holly

"They're fetching in ivy and holly
And putting it this way and that.
I simply can't think of the reason,"
Said Si-Si the Siamese cat.

"They're pinning up lanterns and streamers.
There's mistletoe over the door.
They've brought in a tree from the garden.
I do wish I knew what it's for.

"It's covered with little glass candles
That go on and off without stop.
They've put it to stand in a corner
And tied up a fairy on top.

"They're stringing bright cards by the dozen
And letting them hang in a row.
Some people outside in the roadway
Are singing a song in the snow.

"I saw all the children write letters
And – I'm not at all sure this was wise –
They posted each one up the chimney.
I couldn't believe my own eyes.

"What on earth, in the middle of winter,
Does the family think it is at?
Won't somebody come and tell me?"
Said Si-Si the Siamese cat.

Charles Causley

- **What is the poet saying about the things people do at Christmas?**
- **Explain how the poet expresses his views about Christmas preparations.**

Teachers' note Ask the children if they find the poem funny, and why. What explanations would they give to the cat? Let them consider if these explanations make sense in relation to the Christian celebration of Christmas. What do they notice?

Developing Literacy
Poetry Compendium:
Ages 7–11
© A & C BLACK

Layers of meaning

• **Write a summary of what happens in the poem.**

_____

_____

_____

_____

_____

_____

In This City

In this city, perhaps a street.
In this street, perhaps a house.
In this house, perhaps a room.
And in this room a woman sitting,
Sitting in the darkness, sitting and crying
For someone who has just gone through the door
And who has just switched off the light
Forgetting she was there.

Alan Brownjohn

• **Why is the woman crying?**

> Think about just that one occasion.

_____

_____

You have explained the | literal meaning | **of the poem.**

• **What deeper meaning does it have?**

> Is that the only time the woman cried? Is there another reason for her to be sad?

_____

_____

_____

_____

_____

_____

_____

_____

Now try this!

• **Describe how the poet creates the atmosphere of loneliness.**

Teachers' note Read the poem with the children and ask them to describe the picture they imagine and the feelings the poem evokes in them. Ask them to explain how the poet creates that picture and evokes that feeling.

Developing Literacy
Poetry Compendium:
Ages 7–11
© A & C BLACK

A poet's style

Poet _____ **Date(s)** _____

Place of birth _____

Titles of poems read, and subjects	**Poet's views**
	How I can tell
Poetic forms used  Free verse, haiku, tanka, limerick, monologue…	**Poetic devices used** Metaphor, simile, figurative language, kenning…

How the poet uses sound

Rhythm, rhyme, half-rhyme, assonance, alliteration, onomatopoeia…

Teachers' note If necessary, enlarge the page to A3. It could be used as the basis for a class activity on the same poet (perhaps one of those whose work appears in this book), or for the children to write about a poet of their choice. They should explain their answers using examples.

**Developing Literacy
Poetry Compendium:
Ages 7–11
© A & C BLACK**

125

Native American poem

The poem tells a story.

- **What is the story?**

_____

_____

_____

_____

_____

_____

_____

_____

_____

_____

- **How does the poet feel about the name of the state of Alabama?**

_____

_____

_____

- **Why?**

_____

_____

- **Which words tell you this?**

_____

_____

_____

_____

Alabama

My brethren,
among the legends of my people
it is told how a chief,
leading the remnant of his people,
crossed a great river,
and striking his tipi-stake* upon the ground,
exclaimed, "A-la-ba-ma!"
This in our language means
"Here may we rest!"
But he saw not the future.
The white man came:
he and his people could not rest there;
they were driven out,
and in a dark swamp
they were thrust down into the slime
and killed.
The word he so sadly spoke
has given a name to one of the white man's
    states.
There is no spot under those stars
that now smile upon us,
where the Indian can plant his foot
and sigh "A-la-ba-ma."

    Khe-Tha-A-Hi (Eagle Wing)

* **tipi-stake** — a pole to support a tepee

- **Read other Native American poems.**
- **List any information they give about the culture of Native Americans and about their history.**

Now try this!

Teachers' note Read the poem and tell the children that it was written by a Native American poet in the nineteenth century. Discuss what happened during that time to much of the land on which Native American peoples had lived for centuries and to the people themselves. During a shared reading activity, discuss the questions on the activity sheet.

Developing Literacy Poetry Compendium: Ages 7–11 © A & C BLACK

The poet's experience

- **In what kind of place does the poet live?**
- **Circle the words which describe the place.**

  hot   cold   wet   dry

- **Which words in the poem tell you this?**

  _____
  _____
  _____

- **Number each line of the poem.**
- **For each line write how your life is different.**

  1. _____
      _____
  2. _____
      _____
  3. _____
      _____
  4. _____
      _____
  5. _____
      _____
  6. _____
      _____
  7. _____
      _____
  8–9. _____
      _____
  10. _____
      _____ Continue on the back of this page.

Nomadic Poem

my tree the aloe plant
my flower the crack in the cactus
my river there is none in my country
my basaltic universe in the desert
my close circle of camels
my weapon the dagger
my shadow is lanky
survival is my main
endeavour
my scenery the unchanging horizon
the dust stirred up by my
    soles of sheep's hide
the territory always
in front of me
my guide the desert
my book the sky
every evening picked up
my speech each stone
each flint
my dream always the same:
the nomadic child,
in the simplest state of being

Abdourahman A. Waberi

Teachers' note After reading the poem aloud to the children, ask them where they think the poet lives. Do they know the meaning of 'nomadic'? Discuss other nomadic ways of life, including those of people in Britain. Other words in the poem which might need explaining are 'aloe', 'basaltic' and 'endeavour'.

Developing Literacy
Poetry Compendium:
Ages 7–11
© A & C BLACK

127

Your experience

- **Plan a poem to tell someone from another culture about your lifestyle.**

Main ideas

Structure

Line 1

Line 2

Line 3

Line 4

Line 5

Line 6

Line 7

Line 8

> Write the lines in note form.

Final line

> What message do you want to give?

Useful words

Nouns

Verbs

Adjectives

- **Type out your poem.**
- **Read your poem and edit anything which you can improve.**

Now try this!

> Can you think of more expressive words? Can you improve the rhythm? Make the rhythm match the ideas.

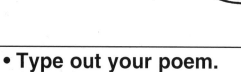

Teachers' note Discuss the words used in the poem on page 127: they give a clear picture of what can be seen in the desert and of the heat, dryness and dust. Read the poem aloud and ask the children to comment on the rhythm: it is a slow, walking pace. What rhythm matches their own lives? (cars, quick-moving television programmes and computer games and so on)

**Developing Literacy
Poetry Compendium:
Ages 7–11
© A & C BLACK**